W9-BFN-487

THE
EXISTENTIALIST'S
SURVIVAL GUIDE

THE
EXISTENTIALIST'S
SURVIVAL GUIDE

How to Live Authentically
in an Inauthentic Age

Gordon Marino, PhD

HarperOne
An Imprint of HarperCollins*Publishers*

HarperOne

Some names have been changed in this book to protect people's privacy.

THE EXISTENTIALIST'S SURVIVAL GUIDE. Copyright © 2018 by
Gordon Marino. All rights reserved. Printed in the United States
of America. No part of this book may be used or reproduced
in any manner whatsoever without written permission
except in the case of brief quotations embodied in critical
articles and reviews. For information, address HarperCollins
Publishers, 195 Broadway, New York, NY 10007.

HarperCollins books may be purchased for educational, business,
or sales promotional use. For information, please email the
Special Markets Department at SPsales@harpercollins.com.

FIRST EDITION

Designed by Diahann Sturge

Library of Congress Cataloging-in-Publication Data

Names: Marino, Gordon Daniel, 1952– author.
Title: The existentialist's survival guide : how to live authentically in an
inauthentic age / Gordon Marino.
Description: FIRST EDITION. | San Francisco, CA : HarperOne, 2018.
Identifiers: LCCN 2017056610 | ISBN 9780062435989 (hardcover)
Subjects: LCSH: Existentialism.
Classification: LCC B819 .M28 2018 | DDC 142/.78—dc23
LC record available at https://lccn.loc.gov/2017056610

18 19 20 21 22   LSC   10 9 8 7 6 5 4 3 2 1

*This is dedicated
to the one I love—
Susan Ellis Marino*

CONTENTS

INTRODUCTION

I want this to be an honest book. No disrespect to other scribblers and beekeepers of ideas, but honest in the sense that instead of serving up re-rehearsed intellectual history, I want to believe that I have absorbed and can pass along some wisdom from Søren Kierkegaard and other existentialists whom I spent much of my adult life studying. "He who studies with a philosopher," the Stoic Seneca (4BC–AD65) tells us, "should take home with him some good thing every day; he should daily return home a sounder man, or on the way to becoming sounder." The same holds for someone like me who has spent decades walking with Kierkegaard and those who followed him. Either I was made sounder or I was wasting my time. If the former, then I ought to be able to pass on a few nuggets of wisdom, and if the latter, then I should remain mum or restrict myself to simply charting the history of existential ideas.

Existentialism is a state in the union of philosophy, and

philosophy is the love of wisdom—as opposed to knowledge—where wisdom might be understood as a pretheoretical understanding of how to live. At the end that was the beginning of this book, I started to feel that, neurotic as I am, I didn't have anything worthwhile to impart, even secondhand. Yes, I know: there is nothing more irksome than an author writing about how hard it was for him or her to write their book. As though the word processor were Aleppo! But when I first sat at the keyboard, the blank page put me on the canvas, or rather in bed. Personally speaking, the attempt to write has always seemed like a confrontation with the void inside me, with my own emptiness.

For all my blessings, I'm a relatively haunted human being. In fact, I would have to place myself on the rather miserable end of the spectrum. Clinically speaking, *I am* a card-carrying depressive. To be fair to myself, I have tried to be a kind person. At least since my borderline-criminal days, I have made substantial efforts to nurture the lives of my students and others, but I am no more a moral hero or sage than I am a contended individual who sleeps soundly and rises in the morning eager to embrace the promises of the day.

My aim in this book is to articulate the life-enhancing insights of the existentialists. And yet their shimmering genius aside, the cast of characters introduced in these pages do not have much better grades on the happiness or moral curve than I do. In truth, to a man and woman, the existentialists are a veritable cadre of neurotics. So, who are they—or me, their apostle—to pass along life prescriptions?

At this juncture, you would be right to prepare for an "on the other hand" or "but still," as in *although I have undermined the very idea of this book, please read on*! Well, you're right: there is a "but still," for all my foibles and problems the existentialists, and Søren Kierkegaard (1813–1855) in particular, helped me to endure. At the risk of seeming histrionic, there was a time when Kierkegaard grabbed me by the shoulder and pulled me back from the crossbeam and rope.

Kierkegaard, Nietzsche, Dostoyevsky, and other existentialist thinkers faced life unblinkered and were nevertheless able to lead authentic lives and keep their heads and hearts intact. More than any other group of philosophers, they understood what we are up against in ourselves, that is, moods such as anxiety, depression, and the fear of death. Today, these inner perturbations are usually classified in medicalizing terms. But in their own inimitable, indirect manner, the existentialists remind of us of another perspective on these and other troublesome emotions. In the pages that follow, I will try to recover those reminders.

Kierkegaard, Nietzsche, Dostoyevsky, and other existentialist thinkers faced life unblinkered and were nevertheless able to lead authentic lives and keep their hearts intact.

I am sure there are readers familiar with that exclamation point of an expression "existential threat," but unfamiliar with existentialism. For those who might be tilting their heads, asking, "What is existentialism?" a survey of the movement is in order.

Existentialists have been perennially concerned with questions about the very meaning of life, questions that tend to come to the fore when we have become unmoored from our everyday anchorage.

The existentialism that helped sustain me is personal in nature. Representatives of this approach think about existence from the inside out, from a first-person perspective. There is much dispute about the roster of this motley crew of thinkers. With the exception of Jean-Paul Sartre (1905–1980), who was the only one to accept the label and only for a short period at that, scholars cannot agree on an official muster list. For instance, I edited *Existentialism: The Essential Writings*, an anthology that included Albert Camus (1913–1960), who, for reasons to be discussed, seemed a no-brainer, and appears in virtually every such collection. Then I thumbed through David Cooper's excellent *Existentialism*, only to learn that the venerable professor denies that Camus is an existentialist because "unlike the rest of our writers, it is not at all his aim to reduce or overcome a sense of alienation or separateness from the world."[1] Strange, because I would have thought that the sheer attempt to articulate this sense of alienation would have been enough to warrant membership in the club.

Further complicating the issue, many of the writers classified under that heading did not in any way think of themselves as philosophers, even though for the most part you'll only find courses on existentialism in philosophy departments. For instance, it would be fair to tab Henry David Thoreau (1817–1862), a contemporary of Kierkegaard, an existentialist even though he is rarely included as one in anthologies or course syllabi.

Though we are without a body of unifying creedal convictions, a set of themes links this diverse group of intellectual pirates. Existentialists have been perennially concerned with questions about the very meaning of life, questions that tend to come to the fore when we have become unmoored from our everyday anchorage. It has been argued[2] that the roots of existentialism were planted as science began to displace faith in what Max Weber termed "the disenchantment of nature." Blame it on Copernicus, who awoke humankind from the dream that the Garden of Eden sits at the center of the earth, earth at the center of the universe with God out there watching the play of human history as though in a theater. Another cause for existential head scratching was the emergence of nation-states in Western Europe, which brought with it the breakdown of the tidy feudal ordering of society, where everyone understood his or her place both in the cosmos and society.

In the modern era, periods of cataclysms have always been a boon to existentialism. Following the abattoir of the First World War, many turned to writers who grasped that life was not dictated by reason, to help them understand, or at least come to grips with, the madness. Interest in existentialism rocketed after World War II and the Holocaust, when humankind once again proved what it is capable of.

And yet, in the mid-twentieth century, at the same time that existentialism was gaining popularity, analytic philosophy ruled the roost in Anglo-American universities. This mode of inquiry developed on the back of logical positivism, a movement that began in Austria with Rudolf Carnap and the conviction that any proposition that was not testable was not worth thinking about. Advances in formal logic also gave a fillip to this hard-nosed mentality, one that placed maniacal stress on logical form and clarity.

If we cleave to the biblical distinction between word and spirit, the spirit of the analytic philosophy was to cleanse philosophy of anything that smacked of metaphysics, unanswerable questions about the nature and foundations of being itself. So far as the fundamentalists of this school of thought were concerned, anything that could not be defined clearly was mumbo jumbo better left alone or to the poets.

I recall a graduate seminar at the University of Pennsylvania, a bastion of analytic philosophy in the early 1980s. Before the beginning of one class, our renowned professor read aloud a sentence from Kierkegaard, a sentence that will reappear more than once in the pages to follow. It is a sentence that encapsulates the leitmotif of this book: "The self is a relation that relates itself to itself or is the relation's relating itself to itself in the relation."[3] Putting down the text, he chuckled and wondered aloud with a tinge of genuine pity, "How could any reasonable person take this spaghetti plate full of words seriously?" Even though I was a fledgling and largely closeted student of the Dane at the time, I couldn't deny that the spaghetti image was so compelling that even Kierkegaard might have cracked a smile over it.

If there was one judgment that united existentialists it was an antipathy toward academic philosophy, with the notable exception of Professor Martin Heidegger (1889–1976). Though he took the equivalent of his doctorate in theology, Kierkegaard was never a professor. In fact, he expressed nothing but disdain for the academicians whom he perceived to be constructing castles of abstractions while living in doghouses next door. Kierkegaard dismissed professors as tapeworms who have nothing of their own to say, but feed off the thoughts of more creative spirits. The existential triumvirate of Sartre, de Beauvoir, and Camus were prolific authors who did not draw checks from universities. Nietzsche, the man who very early on resigned his position as a professor at the University of Basel and rightly said of himself, "I am not a man, I am dynamite,"[4] chided those with chalk in hand for their lack of courage and creativity, hurling insults like "conceptual mummifiers" at them.

There are at least two strands of existentialism. Existential phenomenology, one strand, has its taproot in epistemological worries about what we can and cannot know. It stems from the groundbreaking work of Jewish-German philosopher Edmund Husserl (1859–1938). The epiphany that ignited phenomenology emanated from Husserl's teacher Franz Brentano (1838–1917). Brentano observed that, unlike objects in the material world, mental events—ideas, thoughts, and feelings—are intentional; they always refer to something beyond themselves. For instance, the image I have of the pine tree beside my window refers to something outside of consciousness. In contrast, the pine tree itself just is and does not refer to anything. Bluntly stated, ideas point to something where as things themselves, objects, just are.

But how can you be sure that external objects exist when all you can know is the impression and idea of those objects? After all, contact with the world is mediated by ideas and you can't get outside your ideas to check and see if they correspond to things in the so-called real world. This dilemma is what the philosophers call the "ego-centric predicament." In an end run around questions of this sort, Husserl developed phenomenology, a term that derives from the Greek word for "appearance." He implored us to remove our conceptual glasses and see the world afresh. His clarion call was "back to the things themselves." Husserl's intuition was to "bracket" the question of the existence of things and instead concentrate on delivering pure descriptions of the things themselves. After a fashion, Husserl bid us to glimpse the world as children again, without processing it through concepts. A devotee of Husserl, Sartre was both a philosopher in the traditional sense and a writer of fiction. In his novel *Nausea*, Sartre generates many examples of beholding the world à la Husserl, in its raw form. Midway in the book, Roquentin, the protagonist, is staring at the root of a nearby chestnut tree. Roquentin thinks to himself, "This root . . . existed in such a way that I could not explain it. Knotty, inert, nameless, it fascinated me, filled my eyes, brought me back unceasingly to its own existence . . . I saw clearly that you could not pass from its function as a root, as a suction pump, to *that*, to that hard and thick skin of a sea lion, to this oily, callous, stubborn look."[5] The notion of a suction pump might help you grasp what all roots have in common but it does not explain the concrete particular in front of Roquentin, a particular that could be processed many different ways.

Because of his emphasis on concrete existence, Husserl earned a reputation as a forbearer of existentialism. Phenomenologists such as Sartre who followed him were riveted to the task of revealing the very structures of consciousness. In the thicket of his sometimes impenetrable tome *Being and Nothingness*, Sartre describes a man looking through a keyhole to spy on a woman. Suddenly the voyeur has the feeling that someone has come up behind him. In an instant, he is suffused by shame and immediately goes from feeling like a subject to feeling like an object, which, with some elaboration, Sartre assimilates as evidence that our being-with- and being-for-others is an integral aspect of the structure of consciousness.

Heidegger and Sartre were prime practitioners of the phenomenological method, a method not always appreciated by their Anglo-American brethren. Here is an almost random and, believe it or not, relatively straightforward excerpt from Sartre's *Being and Nothingness*:

> [C]onsciousness is an abstraction since it conceals within itself an ontological source in the region of the in-itself, conversely the phenomenon is likewise an abstraction since it must "appear" to consciousness.[6]

Sartre, who goes on in this manner for some six hundred pages, is claiming that consciousness is an abstraction because consciousness appears to itself as an object of consciousness. For my graduate school professors of the analytic persuasion, this sort of talk was, as Ludwig Wittgenstein put it, "language gone on a holiday." Now, existential phenomenologists might have replied to this insult by saying that the desiccated lingo of philosophical academe should get out of its straitjacket and take a holiday!

There is, however, another cadre of existential thinkers, to whom "existential" still implies attending to concrete existence who avoid floating off into abstract theories detached from reality. For the most part, the reflections in this book keep company with Kierkegaard, Leo Tolstoy (1828–1910), Fyodor Dostoyevsky (1821–1881), Miguel de Unamuno (1864–1936), Camus, and other literary exponents of the existential tradition. All else aside, the sheer ability of these writers to move the waters of language and their fierce engagement with the hurly-burly of real life provide a magnet for rapt attention and engagement.

Going back to the pre-Socratics (and still much alive in the dialogues of Plato), there has been an ongoing debate among the lovers of wisdom as to whether wisdom is best transmitted in the form of *mythos*, stories and poems, or in the form of *logos*, explanations and reason. As the reader will witness, the existentialists who inhabit the following pages delightfully combine elements of both poetry and reason. Most of the writers who have helped me to continue putting one foot in front of the other are logical enough, but tend to rely on stories to transmit their insights about how to live.

Søren Kierkegaard, the poet-philosopher or philosopher-poet of this book, possessed scintillating philosophical abilities; however, he primarily considered himself a poet in the Romantic tradition of a Goethe. For all the arguments Kierkegaard stitched into his sprawling authorship, he was more mythos than logos. Almost unique in detecting the question of how to deliver life-altering and -sustaining truths, Kierkegaard invented and practiced what he termed "the method of indirect communication."

Kierkegaard believed that when it came to the essentials in life—say, how to be a righteous and faithful individual—we have all the knowledge we need. Integrity demands many things, but it does not depend on acquiring new knowledge. If—as Bob Dylan teaches—you don't need a weatherman to know which way the wind blows, you surely don't need an ethics professor to teach you the difference between right and wrong. More than anything, what is required is a passionate relationship to our ideas—and even that sounds too flat, too abstract. This is where mythos comes in.

Kierkegaard believed that when it came to the essentials in life—say, how to be a righteous and faithful individual—we have all the knowledge we need. Integrity demands many things, but it does not depend on acquiring new knowledge.

Kierkegaard believed that ethico-religious communication, that is, communication that has to do with our moral and spiritual lives, was not a matter of conveying thought contents but of pricking conscience, of augmenting care for

> Your hunger for truth ought to be a hunger for truths that build you up, that make you a better human being, if not necessarily a happier individual.

the right things. In one of his most poignant journal entries, penned when he was a twenty-one-year-old on vacation, the young Kierkegaard reminds himself, "Only the truth that edifies is the truth for Thee." The hunger for truth ought to be something more than intellectual curiosity; it ought to be a hunger for truths that build you up, that make you a better human being, if not necessarily a happier individual. At the peril of preaching, these are the truths that we need to be *true to* for them to have purchase on our lives.

Talk with people who identify themselves as philosophers and within moments they will demand, "What's your argument?" Plato and his teacher Socrates believed geometrical proofs to be the model for an argument. With existentialism, argument often takes the form of a story or description, in which you either see yourself or you don't.

The great Scottish philosopher David Hume (1711–1776) conjured up mind-boggling puzzles that philosophers have been trying to solve since his death. And yet, at the end of the day, he was content to leave these problems in his study to go and play billiards as though the conundrums he served up were nothing to lose sleep over. In contrast, the existentialists, like the Stoics, regarded philosophy as a way of life. They were deadly serious about their ruminations.

Camus, for example, began his singular philosophical treatise, *The Myth of Sisyphus*, with these welcoming sentences:

> There is but one truly serious philosophical problem, and that is suicide. Judging whether life is or is not worth living amounts to answering the fundamental question of philosophy. All the rest—whether or not the world has three dimensions, whether the mind has nine or twelve categories—comes afterwards. These are games; one must first answer.[7]

Answer what? The question of whether or not life is worth living. It is Shakespeare's, "To be, or not to be?" A line down, the twenty-nine-year-old Camus pokes a finger in the reader's chest, insisting that if the answer is "life is not worth living," then we should—well—kill ourselves. Camus describes life as a collision between human beings who have an innate craving for meaning and a universe that is as indifferent as rock, utterly devoid of meaning. No matter, Camus counsels that we should put the revolver back in the drawer. Consciousness of absurdity is worth the candle, for as Camus pronounces, "There is no fate that cannot be surmounted by scorn" or laughter.

The analytic philosopher Thomas Nagel offered a rebuttal to Camus's philosophy of the absurd. Judging Camus to be a mite hysterical, the unflappable Nagel explains that the experience of the absurd derives from the simple fact that we humans are unique in our capacity to take two different perspectives on our lives—the everyday view in which we go about our business, and another objective vantage point from which we can look at our lives sub specie aeternitatis. From this perspective, the workings of the world seem trivial, much ado about nothing. Perhaps clad in corduroys and with chalk dust on his pants, Professor Nagel prescribes a dash of irony to dispel the disquieting feeling of the absurd.

Again, unlike Hume and Nagel, the existentialists don't quit their questions for a beer or a game of backgammon. In his *Two Ages*, Kierkegaard decrees that the objective thinker is actually a suicide,[8] because we are *actually* spirits, and the person who continuously strives to think about life from a disinterested perspective systematically chokes the self-interest that is the animating force of his or her spirit.

As intimated earlier, the question of meaning is paramount, both in general (as in what is the meaning of life) and in particular. For instance, later in this book, we will find Kierkegaard, writing under the pseudonym Johannes Climacus, reciting a litany of objective facts about death, but then grabbing the reader by the lapels and reminding us that all the facts in the world won't offer a glimpse into the meaning of *what it means that I will die*. With this emphasis on the "I," the scribblers once known for their berets and black attire, were uniquely inside-out first-person thinkers. Thinking from within the coordinates of my own existence earmarks the existential point of view.

As the subtitle of this book indicates, authenticity is a common theme. Thanks, to some degree, to the ever-presence of and pandemic addiction to social media, we live in an era in which appearances seem more important than reality. Today, there is little premium placed on being authentic. For example, I received an email from a friend who was ill and had to cancel lunch. At the bottom of the page were three boxes with alternative automatic responses: "Oh no. Get well soon." "Thanks. I understand." "I hope you feel better soon." In a dither, I scrolled down and tapped the first alternative but I was embarrassed to respond in such an inhuman, inauthentic manner.

Kierkegaard rarely used the term *authenticity* and it was not a virtue Nietzsche lionized. However, it is not surprising that in the late fifties and sixties *authenticity* and *existentialism* would become terms married to each other. After all, existentialists of almost every ilk stressed honesty with oneself, walking your talk, becoming your true self. Novels like *The Catcher in the Rye*, *The Man in the Gray Flannel Suit*, and *Death of a Salesman* attest to the fact that Americans felt as though Big Brother was watching over them in a disguised but powerful demand for conformity. For all our professed individualism, there was a persistent worry about being a phony, about selling your soul so you could land a job with a company that would put your body in the right kind of car.

In 1946, in the most widely circulated essay ever published on the subject, "Existentialism Is a Humanism," Sartre proclaims that for humans "existence precedes essence." Sartre explains that artifacts created by human design are constructed with an aim or purpose. The purpose is the essence of that thing. Sartre says, for example, take a pair of scissors. Scissors are made to cut. That is their essence. But with humans it is entirely different. Sartre has unshakeable faith that we were not created by God with a plan. So for Sartre, we are who we choose to be. We define ourselves by our choices, which, along with freedom, is another theme unifying the existentialists. Some philosophers have chided existentialists for being mere psychologists. There is a measure of truth to this accusation. They take moods and emotions much more seriously than most of the members of the American Philosophical Association. The pre-Socratic philosopher Heraclitus famously said "you can't step into the same river twice"—everything is in flux. Much of the wisdom found in Western philosophy is faceted to the task of forming an inner compass, of finding something that will keep us constant and steady as the outer and inner world continuously shifts.

For philosophers such as Socrates (469/470–399 BC), Baruch Spinoza (1632–1677), and Immanuel Kant (1724–

1804), reason is the compass, and moods threaten to distort our inner needle. Joy, depression, anxiety, and other affects imperil our inner stability. There are, however, philosophers who tip their caps to feelings. Aristotle (384–322 BC), who during the late–Middle Ages was referred to simply as "The Philosopher," maintained that the recipe for being a virtuous individual entails having the right feelings in the right measure at the right time. Hume, of the razor-sharp mind, believed it was the feeling of sympathy, not reason, that gave wings to our better angels.

And yet the existentialists do more than acknowledge the felt aspect of life. They concentrate on the emotions. Kierkegaard, Heidegger, and Sartre argue that moods like anxiety are conveyors of self-understanding. And for Kierkegaard, depression can instruct us in our powerlessness and total dependency on God. Rather than working to override troublesome feelings, the existentialists directly address the likes of anxiety, depression, envy, and guilt. As Sartre's essay notes, the intense focus on discomfiting feelings capable of bending the shape of our lives has invited critics to grouse that existentialism is too negative, too bleak.

Of course, most of us can be good Samaritans when it is nothing but green lights, but that is not how life usually goes. I once spoke with a young athlete who, crestfallen, confided that she had just been diagnosed with rheumatoid arthritis. Much of her identity and her ways of coping with anxiety had been built around having six-pack abs and sweating it out. Not being able to push herself as much physically is not the end of the world, but she will surely have to struggle to sustain a kind heart in the midst of her anger, her disappointment, and the anxiety that she can no longer leave behind in the weight room.

Saint Paul spoke of the "groaning of existence." Our cast of thinkers recognize that our lives have everything to do with how we absorb the inevitable blows of life.

Once again, the existentialism that was my lifeline is a first-person way of thinking. For that reason, it seems only appropriate to briefly describe the personal circumstances in which Kierkegaard and company became my walking partners.

Saint Paul spoke of the "groaning of existence." Our cast of thinkers recognize that our lives have everything to do with how we absorb the inevitable blows of life.

I grew up in a house of shouts, the clink of ice followed by Friday- and maybe Wednesday-night fights between my parents. One night my brother was just in time to stop my mother from stabbing my besotted father in the chest. Many people have overcome much higher obstacles. After all, there was no question of the love that my warring parents had for their children and of the sacrifices that they were willing to make for us. Nevertheless, growing up in a domestic battleground did not do a lot for me.

I was always in trouble in school and sometimes with the police, but as a young man in the early 1970s, I had just enough prowess in the pigskin arts to get recruited by Bowling Green State University, a Division I football program. Success on the diamond and gridiron were some of the few things that could put a little bounce in the step of my melancholic father. Pitching a no-hitter or scoring a touchdown were accomplishments that made me feel valued by him. And make no mistake about it, it is hard to grow in life without the sunlight of validation.

In my freshman year, thanks to a magician of a professor named Serge Kappler, I became enthralled by philosophy, Socrates, in particular. Socrates was famous for the claim that the unexamined life is not worth living, but more than that, the Socrates of the *Apology* seemed to believe that it was equally exigent to examine everyone and everything. For me, Socrates's dialectical method of interrogation, question, answer, question was like a new toy. Somewhat childishly, I brought it everywhere, even to the sidelines at practice. One afternoon, on a Tuesday after a loss, our freshman coach tried to jack us up and started screaming, "I want you to go out there and hurt somebody." He was a kind enough man, and I am sure he only meant "hit somebody," but I took him literally. Fancying myself a Socrates in a football helmet, I asked, "Coach, why would you want us to hurt someone?" He rolled his eyes, tapped his clipboard on his leg, and walked away.

During the second semester, Professor Kappler took me aside and told me he believed that I was an intelligent and creative student with a knack for philosophy, but I needed to train my mind with the rigor I was accustomed to in sports. Only in his midtwenties, the recently minted PhD could see that my train was running off the rails. In philosophy classes I acted like a bully in a barroom. Run-ins with campus police were becoming routine. Most academics would have discreetly brushed me off as a stereotypical jock. Instead, Serge, as I was invited to call him, trekked over to the administration building to check my high school records and test scores. He frequently had me over to his house, and though I was only a first-year student, he permitted me to participate in a graduate seminar on Plato. It took some doing, but eventually Serge helped me transfer to Columbia University.

I was an angry and insecure teenager from the Jersey Shore with bad habits. I had never lived in New York, and for an immature and imbalanced nineteen-year-old who could put on a good front as an urban pirate, I was a kid in a candy store of alcohol, drugs, and even violence. I had boxed in New Jersey as a teen, and rather than take advantage of the chance to build some mental muscle at Columbia, I was intimidated by my Ivy League classmates and retreated to the pain and sweat parlors of New York's boxing gyms.

After a sparring session in which I more than held my own against a finalist in the NYC Golden Gloves, the manager of the gym signed me to a professional boxing contract. The April night that I signed, I was a man in full, striding down Broadway like John Travolta in *Saturday Night Fever*. A petite coed with long auburn hair and gimlet eyes sashayed by in the opposite direction. As the blues song puts it, she "walked like she had oil wells in her backyard." I did a cartoonlike double take. She wheeled into a Baskin-Robbins, and I was right behind her. As she was waiting to be served, I sidled up to her and in my best James Dean voice said, "I'm going to marry you." I don't recall her exact response but "f off" was the general idea.

As the reader of this fractured fairy tale might have anticipated, a couple of years later we were married. I was unstable. Nikki had her own bevy of demonettes and they were not playing around. There was no limit to what Nikki could do to hurt herself. She was a cutter, but that wasn't all. One night she was enraged to overhear a call from a former girlfriend of mine, and though Nikki was only ninety-eight pounds, she chugged a pint of bourbon in seconds. Not long after, I took it upon myself to separate her from some of her associates who were heavily involved in the drug trade. At three or four in the morning, when she was blitzed in some basement, unaware of how she landed there, she would call

me high and hoot, "Jim Dandy to the rescue." Not knowing what I was getting into, I would go over to fetch her.
One time this involved banging on the door of a local drug
dealer who, were it not for the fact that he thought I was an
undercover cop, would have surely put a deadly ending to
my Travis Bickle charade.

On another night, Nikki was in a dive, sitting at a big
glass-covered table with a posse of minor desperados. One
of them made a snotty remark. I immediately flipped the
table over on them, shattered the glass, and started a war,
which only ended when the bartender pulled out a .45 on me.
By this time, I was so far down the drama rabbit hole that
the black, shiny barrel pointed at my head was just barely
enough to convince me to back off.

Meanwhile, aside from a couple of independent studies, I barely showed up to class at Columbia, and when I
did I was absent while present. Academically I felt as though
I were in over my head, so as if to compensate, I took a
childish pride in my physicality. I would come to seminars
wearing sleeveless T-shirts and the bling of a heavy silver
chain around my neck. Sometimes I arrived in class with
two black eyes earned sparring with some heavyweight or
light heavyweight contender. The bruises gave me a certain
cachet, but as a kind of freak show. When I said something
in seminar that was modestly intelligent, my classmates reacted with surprise. During break, the other seniors would
casually chat about choosing between graduate school at

Harvard or Princeton, or about the law school they would be attending. By the end of my final semester at Columbia, I was lost in the badlands. I had no idea what I would be doing or even wanted to do. It was all street theater and minidramas with Nikki. I was a serious substance abuser who, this side of heroin, would take almost anything to mute the voices behind my brows, usually with prescription drugs, sometimes stealthily filched from the sample drawers at the mental health clinic.

After five years, I was approaching graduation. Existentially speaking, I was at sea and didn't know what to do, so like a somnambulist I mindlessly applied to graduate school. Out of touch, I handwrote applications to some of the premier doctoral programs in philosophy and in return received nothing but skimpy envelopes of rejection letters.

My life was so splintered that it is a strain to put the shards of memory together into a coherent narrative. I floundered at odd jobs in construction, as a mover, a clerical assistant, and a bouncer. My only claim to fame that year was that I filled in for Jake LaMotta at a mobbed-up topless bar in Times Square when Jake went to Hollywood to help Robert De Niro play him in *Raging Bull*.

I don't know whether I had a passion for philosophy or was just sticking with what was familiar. Most likely it was a mix of both, but on my second try I was admitted into a doctoral program at the University of Pennsylvania. There was an air of excitement and hope. Nikki was clean, in treatment, and earning a master's degree in education. We made grown-up plans. She would finish her studies in New York, and I would paddle toward my doctorate in philosophy in Philadelphia. The plan was to get together on weekends. It seemed as though something good, something promising was about to happen. Maybe a quasi-normal life was possible after all.

We took out loans and found a cozy apartment on tree-lined West Philly street. There was a fireplace, white lace curtains. Nikki's late grandfather was a famous heart doctor, and her grandmother vouchsafed us his massive mahogany desk with a glass covering, not unlike the one I smashed at the bar. I put it in the room with the fireplace and a comfy, blue reading chair that came down from my beloved Italian nonna. A pipe and slippers were all I needed. But as always, a foot was about to crash through the door—this time, my own.

On the first day of graduate studies at Penn, I was as nervous as a kindergartener. No more bling and T-shirts, I put on my khaki pants, stuck a pen in the pocket of my Oxford cloth shirt, and made my way to campus. It was a class in epistemology, the theory of knowledge. The other first-year grad students seemed so self-assured. Fifteen minutes into the seminar they were piping in with abstruse references and rehearsed arguments. As the big hand on the clock swept along, the thought began ticking that I was just a poseur, that I had no business in grad school. After a dizzying two-hour session, I shuffled around campus in a daze and then impulsively went to the registrar's office and withdrew from the university, promising myself that I would soon return when I was better prepared. And ultimately I did just that.

I called Nikki to tell her what I had done. When I squeaked open the door to our apartment, she was effectively catatonic. "Nikki! Nikki!" I pleaded. "It's all right. I have it all figured out." She didn't move an inch. I gently grabbed her hands and tried to explain. She was barely blinking. Then, out of nowhere, like some three-hundred-pound barroom brawler, she stood up and flipped the dining room table over, breaking the antique vase that was on it. An hour later, she left with the finality of a door slamming shut in the wind. Before departing, she made it plain that she wasn't going to talk with me anymore or renegotiate our relationship. She was weak in some ways, but there was also something steely about her. She kept her word about not talking anymore. The only negotiation that was going to take place was me trying to internally negotiate this loss on my own.

For almost two years I was one of the walking dead, in and out of the hospital with excessive drinking and drug use. I wasn't selective about which pills I would ingest. I gobbled handfuls. Sometimes in company I would show off by tossing valium in the air and catching those blue 10 mg tabs as though I were a seal. If one night I happened to get my pharmaceutical signals crossed and rode those pills out of existence, so be it.

Kierkegaard observed that, from a worldly point of view, despair seems like it is over *something*, like losing a spouse or not achieving your dream. But it only seems that way. As I will later explain, Kierkegaard taught that despair is always despair over the self, as in I don't want to be myself, or I don't want to be this self. When Nikki vanished, I was stuck with a self that felt like a stinking drunk sleeping on my shoulder on a long bus ride. I was hospitalized at St. Luke's in Manhattan for depression. On the day I was released, I was given a prescription for MAO inhibitors and sternly warned, "Do not drink red wine with this drug!" A friend picked me up at the Upper West Side hospital. Before going a block, I insisted that we stop at a liquor store, where I bought a bottle of red wine and downed it. My unconscious still had dark plans for me.

I was faltering, and after a brief stint living with my parents in New Jersey I went to stay with my older brother Tom in Maine. There, I would park for hours, staring into a space occupied by images of hangings and other suicidal delights. On a blustery, gray winter afternoon, I was sitting on the floor in his cellar and peering over the lip of doom. Teary-eyed, my tender and honest brother put his palm on my shoulder and asked what I wanted him to do with my things if I took my life. A few days later, a zombie of sadness, I returned to my parents' home.

One morning, my father drove me to New York for an appointment with Dr. Beatrice Beebe, a therapist I had been seeing for the past five years. If not for this bodhisattva of a shrink and my existentialist counselors, I would probably have accidentally on purpose slipped out of existence and I certainly would not be preparing to teach tomorrow. Her glimmering insights aside, Dr. Beebe taught me about the matchless healing power of relationships, something easily forgotten in an era of pharmaceutical fundamentalism.

That day, my father and I were early, so he dropped me off at a coffee shop, which was also a used bookstore. Numbly, I started browsing through the shelves, as though remembering a time when I had an intellectual life, when I had a life. I caught sight of a dusty blue-and-gray-covered text. I opened and read from Kierkegaard's *Works of Love*:

> If it were so, as conceited sagacity, proud of not being deceived, thinks, that we should believe nothing that we cannot see with our physical eyes, then we first and foremost ought to give up believing in love. If we were to do so and do it out of fear lest we be deceived, would we not then be deceived? We can, of course, be deceived in many ways. We can be deceived by believing what is untrue, but we certainly are also deceived by not believing what is true.[9]

I am not sure why, but it was a page of light. As though it were only natural, I slipped the book under my coat and walked out to my therapy session. Later that night, I cracked open my purloined philosophy and continued reading.

The writing was both gentle and to the bone. Kierkegaard's words wrapped themselves around me. From the pages of the anxious and melancholy Dane, the idea bubbled up that psychological suffering was not an illness to be passively tolerated, but an action that you could perform either well or poorly. Whether it be from Kierkegaard or the existential psychoanalyst Viktor Frankl, one of the gospel messages to be garnered from existentialism is that suffering can break a person or turn him or her into a rock, but suffering can also provide the impetus for spiritual movement.

From the pages of the anxious and melancholy Dane, the idea bubbled up that psychological suffering was not an illness to be passively tolerated, but an action that you could perform either well or poorly.

I remembered a woman from my stay at St. Luke's. She had opened her wrists a number of times, but despite all her suffering she would bring me a cup of coffee in the morning and offer encouraging words. She could reach through her pain. Maybe that is what I was finding in Kierkegaard—the invocation to reach through the suffering, the anxiety, and inexplicable sadness instead of always looking for the express lane out of that numbing and ever-deepening feeling that nothing matters.

Around the time of this writing, I was flying back from California. Before takeoff there was a little dustup about seating. A cherubic thirtysomething guy with a flattop refused to move out of the aisle until he could exchange with someone for the seat he wanted next to his wife. The line of people boarding was held up, but there he was, with a much less than endearing grin, telling those of us laden with bags and waiting in the aisle, "It always works out." At around the same time, I happened to peer down at my phone at images of Houston and the surrounding area under water from Hurricane Harvey. So far, there were five people dead and the rain was still torrential. No, my friend, it does not always work out.

The existentialists who make up the conversations in this book recognized that things don't always work out for the best. They address life as it is. During the sixties and seventies, a gaggle of authors—such as Ernest Becker, Rollo May, Erik Erikson, and Paul Tillich, all distant students of Kierkegaard—firmly believed that through self-reflection we could make progress as human beings. These once-renowned philosopher-psychologists are now looked upon with a condescending smile for their naïveté. They were true believers in a kind of human progress that went beyond improved functioning and enhanced enjoyment. For all the mindfulness and yoga classes today, we have become more skeptical about a certain kind of personal human progress. We think of depression, anxiety, grief, and other disconcerting emotions as inner disturbances to be doused with pills and adjusted with other forms of lifestyle engineering. The thinkers between these covers do not offer a step-by-step plan for coping with our feelings of inadequacy, or a checklist of behaviors to avoid. Instead of detailing some strategy for assuaging our depression, they might tender advice on how to keep our moral and spiritual bearings when it feels as though we are going under.

At the same time, there are important topics that I could not catch up with in this jog through the terrain of existential ideas. Most troubling for me is the question of whether or not this is a guide for everyone, regardless of skin color or gender? Here I am tapped on the shoulder by Ralph Ellison, author of perhaps the greatest existential novel, *Invisible*

The thinkers between these covers do not offer a step-by-step plan for coping with our feelings of inadequacy, or a checklist of behaviors to avoid. Instead of detailing some strategy for assuaging our depression, they might tender advice on how to keep our moral and spiritual bearings when it feels as though we are going under.

Man. In his masterpiece, Ellison revealed that one of the symptoms of the poison of racism is that it renders people of color invisible. Is becoming yourself (if there is such a thing) the same kind of task for an undocumented Latina hotel maid as it is for a white professor? For reasons that will become clear, Kierkegaard would most likely answer "yes," but I have to disagree with my sage. Finding and becoming yourself has to be a more complicated process for, say, African-Americans than for whites, as African-Americans have to burrow out of the inwardly appropriated suspicious gaze that tracks them up the aisles in the department store, and much, much worse.

There are questions of identity that blacks—and, yes, women—have to grapple with that white men of a particular economic class can simply and safely ignore. I confess that I have grown weary of the terms "people of color" and "white privilege"; but make no mistake about it, being free of the task of fending off other people's stereotypes is at the core of "white privilege." Those of us who enjoy the liberty of not having to ask ourselves about the borderline between our skin color and our core identity sometimes find it hard to understand, feelingly, that we are privy to a space of reflection denied to our brothers and sisters. Perhaps our inability to grasp this essential truth is why we don't yet know how to act upon it.

Though Kierkegaard's bicentennial was in 2013, he and his epigones offer a new window through which to understand ourselves and the feelings that can threaten to uproot our ability to care. In the first leg of this book, I will distill existential insights on how best to understand and relate ourselves to the trials posed by anxiety, depression, despair, and death. In the second leg, I address more positive aspects of existence, namely, authenticity, faith, morality, and love—but with the caveat that these topics also pose daunting challenges.

CHAPTER

1

ANXIETY

Virtually every morning, I am attacked by clawed thoughts: "Has my wife's cancer come back? Will my son have a wreck on his commute? Blip, blip, blip, my tooth hurts. I wonder if I will need that one pulled too. Losing teeth makes me feel so old."

It is a never-ending blizzard of little and big gut-churning worries that seem to make it impossible to be present. An aborning spring day, the trees are exploding, but the only thing I can glimpse is a world that snarls like a pit bull on a short leash. Of course, none of this will prevent me from exchanging niceties with neighbors and even people toward whom I don't feel so nicely. If the proverbial slate fell off the roof today and killed me, no one besides my wife would know that I was a walking haunted house aflame with anxiety. There are times when I have laughingly reminded myself that all the things I imagine happening could not possibly happen. I entertain some of my past fears and try to remind myself that many of the devils I was sure were bearing down on me were just shadows. Then again, I know people who have come down with cancer and heart disease at virtually the same time. And I have had my share of golems leap out of the closet on sunny days. For me, there is always something to be anxious about, and if there weren't, I would probably look for, or most likely invent, some pretext for anxiety.

The Romanian philosopher and aphorist Emil M. Cioran (1911–1995), a veritable Nietzsche on steroids, wrote:

> Anxiety is not provoked: it tries to find a justification for itself, and in order to do so seizes upon anything, the vilest pretexts, to which it clings once it has invented them. . . . [A]nxiety provokes itself, engenders itself, it is "infinite creation."[1]

Cioran is correct. Anxiety is a moveable feast, one that has been understood differently at different times.

In the fifties and sixties, during the cold war years, many Americans would sit at their office desks, roll their pencils in their hands, wondering at one moment whether or not it was worth building a bomb shelter and, in the next, about building a vacation home. A period of robust economic boom, that era was the proverbial best of times and most anxious of times, redolent with fears about the bomb and of bombing out in a time of intense upward mobility. Maybe it was the advances of science and/or the Holocaust, but for a large flock of people, faith in God and sacred order seemed to be nodding off or put to bed. We were on our own and could no longer trust that our lives had a fixed meaning as pieces in a divine galactic puzzle. It was no coincidence that during this era nerve balms like Miltown and, later, Valium started hitting the market.

Anxiety is a moveable feast, one that has been understood differently at different times.

Nor was it a coincidence that existentialism became popular in America during this post–World War II period, christened by the poet W. H. Auden (1907–1973) "the age of anxiety." Back then, there was an intellectual tradition of pondering the meaning of anxiety. For a small sampler, in 1950 the existential psychoanalyst Rollo May published *The Meaning of Anxiety*. A string of related works followed, including his 1969 bestseller *Love and Will*. In 1952, Paul Tillich published *The Courage to Be*, a Kierkegaardian mediation on angst. Then there was Ernest Becker's Pulitzer Prize–winning *The Denial of Death*, and, among scads of other works, a raft of meditations on anxiety from Alan Watts, including *The Wisdom of Insecurity*.

Then Big Pharma and the insurance giants rolled in. Steeped in Marx and Nietzsche, the French philosopher Michel Foucault (1926–1984) taught us the Hegelian lesson that our understanding of ourselves is profoundly influenced by the institutions in which our lives are embedded, in this case the health care industry. Such institutions generate our vocabulary for thinking about our emotional lives. When Christianity held sway, people understood their inner being in terms of sin, temptation, and forgiveness. With what the prescient Philip Rieff (1922–2006) termed the "triumph of the therapeutic," psychoanalysis and related forms of psychotherapy generated another set of terms with which to address ourselves: "Don't be so anal" or "You're in denial." According to Rieff, who as my mentor will be a regular presence in this book, Americans would soon come to regard just about everything as a subject for a class of expert-like therapists offering counsel and workshops on how to think and talk about grief, ethics, race—you name it.

Pharmaceutical companies were not content to hawk medications; they were also marketing psychological disorders themselves. One *Mad Men*–type advertisement depicted a twentysomething woman at a party. Over a series of scenes, it became clear to the viewer that the woman was feeling awkward and self-conscious. Then, just when the self-consciousness became too much to bear, came the suggestion that she was suffering from "social anxiety" disorder, a treatable malady. Soon enough, "social anxiety" was included in the *Diagnostic and Statistical Manual of Mental Disorders (DSM)*, the Bible of psychiatry. Once this happened, psychiatrists and therapists could be reimbursed for their treatment of this disorder, which, of course, included a regimen of medication. But when it came to anxiety, the gospel message was unambiguous and inviting: no need to muck around in your past—you have a "chemical imbalance" which can be adjusted and cured with a pharmaceutical treatment plan.

In other words, when it came to plaguey feelings and thoughts, the new credo was that these were best understood as neurochemical squalls. If the movement had a bumper sticker it might have been WHERE THERE'S A PILL, THERE'S A WAY. Make no mistake about it, some states of mind are the result of organic problems or changes in the brain. Still, it doesn't follow that an endlessly buzzing anxiety about any- and everything is best understood in terms of neurons. This reductionist view collapsed the difference between the cause and meaning of anxiety, as if being able to chemically intervene in a thought process rendered the meaning of that thought process a matter of indifference. Among other things, this brave-new-world position, which ordains doctors and scientists as priests of the inner life, ignores the reality of top-down causation. It is not just changes in neurotransmitters that impact our thoughts and moods. The sword cuts two ways. The mantra of the era is "studies show," and yes, studies attest to top-down causation, to the fact that meditation and therapy impact neurochemistry.

Once, I was chatting with a student after class when our conversation was interrupted with a cell phone call from a dean informing her that she had been accepted with a full scholarship to medical school. In a three-minute conversation, she went from feeling somewhat glum to ecstatic. When she hung up, her cheeks were ruddy and she was almost literally jumping for joy. No doubt, the mere string of words did something to her gray matter. If you have ever received the body blow of a "Dear John" letter, you will not need anyone to prove to you that sentences can have a physical signature, that our understanding is embodied. The right words for the right person can transport you to seventh heaven; the wrong ones can put a knot in your stomach. Even if it could be proven that anxiety was the by-product of neurochemical combustion, it would not follow that the feeling was devoid of significance. Remember: in vino veritas. Alcohol loosens the lips, but the rants that we go on when we are under the influence are not exactly random; they are often revelatory.

For another vignette from the lecture hall, I once had a student come to me pleading for an extension on his paper on account of the fact that he was suffering anxiety attacks. Almost casually, he mentioned that a few weeks before, his parents had divorced, but to hear him tell it, that had nothing to do with his agitated state of mind. There was no use thinking about the divorce. "After all," he told me, "I'm twenty-one and not living at home. It shouldn't bother me that much." As far as he was concerned, reflection was beside the point; all he needed to do was to get his "meds titrated" so that he could get back to functioning on the academic assembly line. For him, anxiety was just a meaningless, disruptive symptom that did not require psychotherapy or even introspection. Was he correct? Is anxiety just a psychic fever? Should we just extinguish anxiety if we can?

Freud proclaimed that if we understood anxiety, "it would be bound to throw a flood light on our whole mental existence." In the early stages, Freud thought of anxiety as the simple by-product of bottled up and repressed sexual wishes. Later, he formulated another theory in which anxiety was cast as an internal signal of danger. This is complex, but consider an example: suppose that whenever a young boy got angry at his mother, she withdrew. Given how intensely a child needs his mother, sudden dramatic withdrawals would be terrifying. By the simple law of association, then, the child, now an adult, will come to experience anger as profound threat and find his ire difficult to acknowledge and admit into consciousness. For Freud, anxiety is an internal danger sign that in effect reads, "Act on this impulse and you are likely to lose the affection of meaningful others." The Freudian strategy, which has largely been taken over by therapists who otherwise snicker at Freud, would be to uncover those initial experiences and learn that while it might have been reasonable to feel anxious about being angry as a child, it is no longer appropriate. For Freud, anxiety is not just a surge of chemicals; it is a capsulized version of experience, a piece of intimate knowledge about the self.

Philosophers have not always taken anxiety seriously, or rather they have tended to regard it as a disruptive by-product of an untamed mind. Without distinguishing between anxiety and fear, the rationalist Spinoza wrote, "Fear arises from a weakness of mind and therefore does not appertain to the use of reason." Those suffering from anxiety are anxious because they have not adequately developed the mental muscle to deal with anxiety. They are either out of touch with reality or unable to accept it. Historically, many philosophers seem to believe that anxiety does nothing more than throw a wrench in the machinery of reason. The majority of psychiatrists seem to share this belief today.

Philosophers have not always taken anxiety seriously, or rather they have tended to regard it as a disruptive by-product of an untamed mind.

And then there is that hybrid author, poet, theologian, philosopher Søren Kierkegaard. Along with his twenty-two volumes of published work, Kierkegaard kept an endless set of journals, which he ultimately intended for public consumption. In his diaries, he took copious notes on the anxiety that swarmed behind his dancing blue eyes. In one such entry from 1844, Kierkegaard confided, "These days I suffer very much from a mute disquietude of thought. I am enveloped in anxiety; I cannot even say what it is that I cannot understand."[2] Four years later, Kierkegaard scribbled this note to himself, "It is appalling to think even for one single moment about the dark background of my life right from its earliest beginning. The anxiety with which my father filled my soul, his own frightful depression, a lot of which I cannot even write down."[3]

Penned in 1844, Kierkegaard's groundbreaking study *The Concept of Anxiety* hypnotized an august cadre of philosophers, theologians, and writers, and, a century later, formed the bedrock of existential psychoanalysis. Although Kierkegaard wrote many edifying works in his own name, the books that immortalized him such as *Fear and Trembling*, *Either/Or*, *The Sickness unto Death*, and *Concluding Unscientific Postscript*, were all written under pseudonyms. There is an ongoing scholarly debate about how to interpret the meaning of these noms de plumes; however, I suggest that each pseudonym represents a different perspective on life. *The Concept of Anxiety* is signed by Vigilius Haufniensis, a self-proclaimed psychologist and the watchman of the harbor. (Kierkegaard's hometown, Copenhagen, is a harbor town par excellence.) Unlike most members of the philosophy guild, Kierkegaard did not reduce the emotions to inner clouds obscuring the beatific light of reason. For Kierkegaard, anxiety has a cognitive component. It helps us to know ourselves. It informs us that we are beings who have choices, who choose ourselves. Thus, the existential shibboleth formulated by Sartre—that for humans and humans alone, "existence precedes essence"; that is, we first come into existence and only then define ourselves through our choices. If that is not enough to make you grind your teeth, I don't know what is.

Although he doesn't identify anxiety with any particular physical phenomena, such as sweaty palms or a rapid heartbeat, Kierkegaard describes anxiety as "the dizziness of freedom." In anxiety I can come to understand that I am free, that I am a creature fraught through and through with possibilities. That freedom, the necessity to constantly make choices, to realize this possibility and close down another, is a font of anxiety. The example that Sartre uses to illustrate this point is one of standing on a cliff edge. Looking over the lip of a thousand-foot drop, our stomachs quiver, we experience anxiety, not because we are in danger of falling but because we feel that we have the freedom to leap.

Some commentators grumble that what Kierkegaard meant by anxiety is something alien to the recurrent feelings that we fill our prescriptions to assuage. However we parse our inner life, Kierkegaard would not have been baffled by our understanding of our unease. Does this journal entry sound as though it were written by someone unfamiliar with the feelings that steer us to the mental health clinic?

> What is it that binds me? . . . I, too, am bound . . . by a chain formed of gloomy fancies, of alarming dreams, of troubled thoughts, of fearful presentiments, of inexplicable anxieties. This chain is "very flexible, soft as silk, yields to the most powerful strain, and cannot be torn apart."[4]

Kierkegaard acknowledged that anxiety is a feeling unlike others. As the psychotherapist Rollo May, a devoted student of Kierkegaard, explained, anxiety "is not a peripheral threat that I can take or leave; . . . it is always a threat

---

Looking over the lip of a thousand-foot drop, we experience anxiety, not because we are in danger of falling but because we feel that we have the freedom to leap.

---

to the foundation, to the center of my existence." Fear is something that we can put a label on and objectify—as in, I am afraid to go to the doctor for a stress test. But as May puts it, "in greater or lesser degree anxiety overwhelms the person's awareness of existence, blots out the sense of time . . . attacks the center of one's being."

Unlike other moods and emotions, anxiety is something that can inhabit us without betraying its presence. Kierkegaard sighs:

> Deepest within every person there is nonetheless an anxiety about being alone in the world, forgotten by God, overlooked among the millions and millions in this enormous household. People keep this anxiety at bay by looking at the many people around them, who are related to them as family and friend; . . . one scarcely dare think about how one would feel if all these were taken away.[5]

Kierkegaard depicts anxiety from diverse angles, but like another depth psychologist, he discerned that we have our defenses against anxiety, our ways of deflecting it. In the quote above, he is using *fear* and *anxiety* interchangeably, but again, deep within every individual there is an anxiety that threatens to overrun us, an anxiety that we are primed to flee by disguising it as another feeling. Remember, "people keep this anxiety at bay by looking at the many people

around them" and perhaps calming their spirits by reminding themselves that relatively speaking, they are faring well.
There are other ways of putting the reins on anxiety. Maybe
we frantically weed the garden, obsess about exercise goals
like cycling eighty miles per week, paint and then repaint
the house—constantly trying to make sure that everything
is in order, that we are in control. Anxiety, however, is always about possibility. Kierkegaard notes, "When shrewdness has completed its innumerable calculations, when the
game is won—then anxiety comes, even before the game in
actuality has been lost or won . . . shrewdness becomes help-
less and its most clever combinations vanish like a witticism
compared with the case that anxiety forms with the omni-
potence of possibility."[6] Get it all figured out and there is
always something else to be anxious about. Anxiety is about
the future, and, because of this, it impedes our ability to live
in the moment.

Borrowing extensively from Kierkegaard, Heidegger
agreed that anxiety is a teacher, that it discloses something
of paramount importance to us about our humanity. It grabs
us from within and separates us from the world, makes us
homesick for that feeling of being in the swing of things.

Anxiety is about the future, and, because of this, it impedes our ability to live in the moment.

On a late night, I was walking my dogs. The nacre moon was full. Shimmering stars were slowly sailing across the obsidian sky. A cool, refreshing breeze was soughing through leafy maples. It was a once-in-a-summer summer evening. Intellectually, I could acknowledge the magic of the hour, but anxiety had come for a visit. As far as I was concerned, it might as well have been a gray, sleeting December afternoon. That dislodged feeling, says Heidegger, ultimately helps us secure our identities as authentic individuals separate from the crowd. Anxiety extracts us from what Heidegger sometimes refers to as the "They," but then enables us to return to our communal life as authentic individuals no longer lost in and defined by the crowd.

"Anxiety," Kierkegaard explains, "is *a sympathetic antipathy* and *antipathetic sympathy*."[7] In his journals, Kierkegaard wrote more straightforwardly, "Anxiety is a desire for what one fears . . . an alien power which grips the individual, and yet one cannot tear himself free from it and does not want to, for one fears, but what he fears he desires. Anxiety makes the individual powerless."[8] Anxiety is something that we produce—after all, it is a function of our freedom. Yet it feels as though it is something coming from the outside; hence the expression "anxiety attack." Anxiety is like a horror movie, one that prompts us to put our palms over our eyes, but then we peek through our fingers anyhow, a simultaneous attraction and repulsion. "In observing children," Kierkegaard writes, "one will discover this anxiety intimated more particularly as a seeking for the adventurous, the monstrous, and the enigmatic."[9]

I fear that references to pugilism will seem discordant with a discussion of Kierkegaard and Heidegger, so please bear with me. I witness frequent examples of sympathetic antipathy and antipathetic sympathy in my second career as a boxing trainer. Next to everyone wants to be a tough guy. Eager youngsters come to me all the time, passionately declaring, "I want to be a boxer. I promise I'll be there every day." As long as we are just going through the moves and learning the basics, the ardent desire remains. But then, usually after their first or second sparring session, after taking a couple of shots to the snoot and having an illusion or two caved in, they conjure up some excuse and disappear. As if that weren't vexing enough, a couple of months later, the urge rumbles back, and they contact me again about returning to the gym. From a Kierkegaardian perspective, anxiety is an approach-avoidance conflict, one in which we are boxing with ourselves, or more specifically, sparring with the intimidating prospect of exercising our freedom and realizing the possibility of becoming our true selves.

When you lurch out of a deep slumber at 4:30 a.m. and anxieties are mercilessly twittering in your head like birds in the bushes outside your window, the idea that anxiety has *anything* to do with becoming your true self seems laughable. Actually, anxiety aside, it is difficult enough to believe in the kind of self to which Kierkegaard beckons us. Even though we live in an age of fanatical self-devotion and improvement, the concept of the self is on the ropes, every bit as much as the concept of the soul. On an everyday level, we cannot help but believe that we are selves. Nevertheless, it seems impossibly difficult to identify anything about ourselves that remains the same over the course of a lifetime. Philosophers tab this the "problem of personal identity," and scant few of them would argue that we have a reasonable basis for claiming that we have a substantive identity over time. Hume contended that there is no sense datum on which to ground the idea of an enduring self. On his account, when we refer to ourselves, we point only to a "bundle of perceptions."

From a Kierkegaardian perspective, anxiety is an approach-avoidance conflict, one in which we are boxing with ourselves, or more specifically, sparring with the intimidating prospect of exercising our freedom and realizing the possibility of becoming our true selves.

The modern notion of the self is one of a fragmented entity. It requires something close to faith to hold fast to the idea that amid all the changes that we endure over a lifetime, there is something that remains the same. At sixty-plus, I sometimes roll my eyes when I look in the mirror as if to ask, Is that really you, I mean me? John Locke (1632–1704) suggested that personal identity consists of continuity in our memories, but the Grand Canyon–size gaps in the internal record of our lives makes that suggestion seem dubious. Some contemporary philosophers unpack personal identity in narrative terms, as though the self were a story that the self told itself about itself. For Zen Buddhists, there is a ladder of illusions that we must scale and overcome to achieve enlightenment. In the end, you need to understand the empty mirror; you need to get over yourself, to get over the very idea that you are a self. While Kierkegaard shares many affinities with Buddhist thinkers, he nevertheless gestures in the opposite direction toward a strong belief in the self.

For Kierkegaard, it is almost as if the potential to become a self, a term he uses synonymously with *spirit*, announces itself to itself in the experience of anxiety. What is the proof, the evidence for, the anxiety/self connection? It is a subjective experience, but not the kind that could be tested in a controlled experiment. After all, how would we operationally define the "true self"? And yet I suppose that if we restricted our corpus of beliefs to those that could only be established on the basis of empirical evidence, we would be left with a narrow set of convictions. Those who have chosen the either-or of only bowing to the verdicts of science would surely surrender belief in the self in any strong Kierkegaardian sense of the term.

For Kierkegaard, humans are uniquely paradoxical creatures, walking and talking contradictions. We are a synthesis of the temporal and eternal, the finite and the infinite, necessity and possibility. However, we are not just a synthesis—we are charged with the thorny task of relating these two aspects of ourselves to one another. We have an idea of ourselves as infinite and ongoing, and another as a purely finite creature. We have dreams (possibility) about what we could be, and then there are the facts of our concrete situation (necessity). Unlike other creatures, humans have the task of integrating these aspects of the self. It is as though an ontological possibility hovers over us as an anxiety-inducing responsibility.

However, I have already emphasized that one of the essential qualities of existentialists is that they are realists. If it feels as though anxiety is robbing you of your life, you probably won't care to hear existential yak-yak about "ontological possibilities." Considering that this was not Kierkegaard's vocabulary, what then does he have to teach us concerning the ever-present problem of anxiety? Kierkegaard can surely be read as affirming that anxiety is a definitive sign that we are selves. He assures, "Anxiety . . . is an expression of the perfection of human nature"; it is "the homesickness of earthly life for the higher." The positive aspects of feeling like you are going to jump out of your skin are hard to fathom, but consider self-consciousness. It is often unpleasant and worse, and yet to lack it would be to be less than human.

No therapist is he; Kierkegaard does not try to formulate techniques for calming our jitters. He does, however, recommend that we try to stay at our post, to sit with the onslaughts of the sense that everything is becoming unhinged. One of the mistaken ways we respond to the dizzying feeling is to attempt to steady ourselves by converting existential anxiety into a revolving worry about this or that finite concern. If I just get such and such a job, we tell ourselves, I'll be all right. If my daughter Jill can just gain admittance to the college she is set upon . . . on and on goes the whirligig of anxieties. On the fictional fix-alls, Kierkegaard comments, "From finitude one can learn much, but not how to be anxious, except in a very mediocre and depraved sense."[10]

There is no need to whip ourselves for our all-too-human finite concerns. As Irvin Yalom, the doyen of existential psychoanalysts, puts it, "that is just the way we are put together." But how to relate to those anxieties? Kierkegaard's existential prescription is that we cultivate the capacity to abide with these unsettling moods, learn to sit on the couch with our fears. Why? Because according to our virtuoso of inwardness, "Whoever has learned to be anxious in the right way has learned the ultimate."[11]

Kierkegaard understood that there are throngs of people who have been crushed by anxiety and/or their endless attempts to escape it. But he is emphatic—anxiety can save us. Just listen to him: "Anxiety is freedom's possibility, and only such anxiety is through faith absolutely educative, because it consumes all finite ends and discovers all their deceptiveness."[12] That is to say, with faith you understand the one thing that you should be anxious about, namely, your relationship to God, and with that anxiety, all your other sources of anxiety become relativized.

Because according to our virtuoso of inwardness, "Whoever has learned to be anxious in the right way has learned the ultimate."

No doubt, the "through faith" will illicit a grimace from many readers. Kierkegaard would disown me for it, but perhaps we can ease the rub of faith by allowing that, if you trust that your task in life is to become an authentic human being, then you will know what you should truly fear—namely, becoming a vacant-eyed, empty suit of an individual. For the person whom anxiety has taught to trust in God, or even in his or her moral self, "[A]nxiety becomes a serving spirit. . . . Then when [anxiety] announces itself, when it cunningly pretends to have invented a new instrument of torture . . . he does not shrink back, and still less does he attempt to hold it off with noise and confusion."[13]

This is not something you are likely to hear from your therapist, but magister Kierkegaard has it that when a serious person feels anxiety scratching at the door, he or she

> bids it welcome, greets it festively, and like Socrates who raised the poison cup, he shuts himself up with it and says as a patient would to the surgeon . . . Now I am ready. Then anxiety enters into his soul and searches out everything and anxiously torments everything finite and petty out of him. . . . So when the individual through anxiety is educated unto faith, anxiety will eradicate precisely what it brings forth itself.[14]

The anxiety that emanates from us and yet seems an alien force animates all sorts of goblins and can often leave us feeling impuissant and completely vulnerable. However, that sense of powerlessness can prod us to trust in God, or if God raises your hackles, trust in the idea that we weren't put on this earth just to play golf and sip martinis on a beach. Kierkegaard is adamant that courage comes when one fear/anxiety drives out another. For instance, a platoon leader on the battlefield might lay in her tent at night fretting about whether or not she has the respect of her troops, but when her squadron is under attack, that anxiety will vanish, pushed aside by the one and only thing to be anxious about—protecting her brothers and sisters in arms.

There is much that I have left out of Kierkegaard's account

of anxiety. The neglected nuances aside, what kind of balm does Kierkegaard provide to the angst-ridden? To reiterate, incubus that it can be, anxiety is not an affliction but the manifestation of our spiritual nature, such that "Only a prosaic stupidity maintains that this [anxiety] is a disorganization," or in modern parlance, an illness. As for the seemingly unflappable individual who boasts that he has never experienced anxiety, Kierkegaard's explanation is to the point: "That is because he is spiritless."

To summarize, Kierkegaard and all those in his lineage prescribe that we make friends with this devilish mood or feeling, for it has unique and fundamental instruction to offer. And yet, if we panic about those feelings of panic, anxiety can be our undoing and sadly enough, the flight from it can become the axis around which our lives orbit, when that axis ought to be the project of becoming our true and authentic self. Kierkegaard discerned lineaments linking anxiety and the next inner obstacles that we will enlist the existentialists to help us surmount, that is, depression and despair.

CHAPTER
2

DEPRESSION AND DESPAIR

At last count, one in eight Americans was being medicated for depression. On the face of it, many of us of the sad countenance don't have anything to moan about, which, if anything, makes us feel worse. We pay someone to mow our backyards and spend hours searching the internet to find the best deal for our next vacation. What's our problem?

Back in the late sixties, my high school principal, whose office I made many trips to, pressed virtually the same question. I don't know where it came from, but on one visit I attempted to excuse my disruptive class behavior by pleading that I was acting up because I was depressed. Puzzled for a moment, the beefy, flat-topped administrator waved me over to his desk. Picking up a pencil, he drew a straight line with an indentation. I had the feeling that he had given this sermonette before, but he explained that the notch was a depression like you might see in the earth. He then leaned back in his chair and concluded, "A depression is a hole, and a hole is nothing. So depression is nothing."

This was a ludicrous equivocation, but I could not argue that at the time. The principal was a veteran of the war in the Pacific, and I must have seemed like a kid who just needed to toughen up and learn to deal with the hard times. Depression is not so simple. As Kierkegaard wrote, "Depression is something real that one does not delete with the stroke of a pen." More than that, Kierkegaard maintained that depression was the signal defect of his own age, the defect "that has robbed us of the courage to command, the courage to obey, the power to act, the confidence to hope."

When you are walking under the black sun,[1] you generally feel like a victim—weak and powerless. No matter what you might think of Freud, who, by the way, was about as far from an existentialist as possible, he was astute in observing that there is a fury beneath the apparent passivity of the depressive, a merciless and relentless rage directed at the self. Among other things, depression is a disturbance in the way that we talk to ourselves. Personally, I connect the funk with being bombarded by debilitating thoughts, thoughts that lift me out of the present and engulf me with a feeling of utter hopelessness, thoughts that even manage to leave me bereft of all curiosity.

One day, I was re-reading a text, preparing to teach my class on existentialism. Somewhere along the page the word *father* loomed up, and I was immediately tumbling down the memory well to my father's burial twenty-five years earlier. Peering out the snow-feathered window, I re-called, it was in December on what felt like the coldest day in my recorded history. I live in Minnesota and yet have never experienced a chill as piercing. It was so blustery that the priest, dressed in purple vestments and a long black coat, had to struggle just to keep his hat on as he read a short passage from the Bible. With the wind madly gusting, I couldn't hear a word he said. My dad didn't go to church. The priest didn't know him from Adam, which meant he was at a glaring loss for some final words. It was evident that Father Whoever couldn't wait to get in his car and back to the warmth of the rectory. A pervasive emptiness seemed

---

Depression is a disturbance in the way that we talk to ourselves. Personally, I connect the funk with being bombarded by debilitating thoughts, thoughts that lift me out of the present and engulf me with a feeling of utter hopelessness, thoughts that even manage to leave me bereft of all curiosity.

---

to enfold everything, an emptiness so profound that it felt as though the devil himself had created it. Back in his salad days, my father was always surrounded by buddies, but only one pal was present when they laid him down.

In a fizzling funk myself, my thoughts kept crawling away from the book I was supposed to be freshening up on, and I started reminiscing about that once-successful businessman, how the breastbone of all his hopes were slowly crushed by depression and decades of trying to douse that depression with Seagram's 7. In the good years, my old man was a classic dresser, Brooks Brothers suits, Oxford cloth shirts; but when the time came to place him in his six-foot office, we had to "borrow" a tie because he had tossed all of his. Wincing as it came to mind, I got to thinking that my mother could have gone out and bought a tie. Instead, she borrowed one from the retired iron worker who lived next door. Borrow? As though we were going to return it!

The connections between ideas zipping through our skulls is a mystery. A few synapses later, I circled back three decades to the autumn afternoon when I cheated on my onetime fiancé, necking with her best friend in a pew of Riverside Church. Grimacing as though from a foul smell, I squinched up my face and literally whispered to myself, "What were you thinking?"

Class started in two hours, but the scourge wouldn't stop; first, various forms of self-flagellation followed by images of doom and disappointment. The beautiful woman whom I love and have been sleeping next to for thirty-five years is a breast cancer survivor. Now it's Parkinson's. We can forget the so-called golden years of retirement. Throughout my adult life, I was always able to do a respectable imitation of a tough guy. After all, I was a boxer and a boxing trainer. No one messed with me. And yet, when it came to being in the ring of life, paying the bills, moving, coping with family ills, Sue had always been the rock. It was no secret to me or my kids. And now with these relentless self-attacks, when I feel like I can't change a light bulb, I'm supposed to be the one to rely on. Good luck.

As though my addled mind can't help but try to figure out what is going on in the engine room, I draw a few deep breaths and try to reflect my way out of the cell. I picture this homunculus in my brain, Mr. Executive Function. I see him rocking back and forth in an office chair up there, unable to understand why he can't stop the self-torture. Psychoanalysts talk about the importance of having an observing ego, a psychological third eye, a part of the self that keeps watch on the inner workings of your mind. In my melancholic case, however, the observing ego has been dragged into the muck that it, that *I*, was supposed to be observing. When the depression reaches a pitch, it is easy to lose all perspective, temporal and otherwise. This is when things get dangerous, when there is no longer any inside that is outside this inner cloud. Instead of reassuring myself "this too shall pass," it seems perfectly rational to conclude, "My father and grandfather succumbed to this. So will I."

Finally, I arrive at my edge, the point where I feel I can't take it anymore. I shuffle into the bathroom and reach into the medicine cabinet, careful to avoid catching myself in the mirror. Like the existentialists, and the stoics long before them, my view has always been that we need to be able to absorb suffering, bear it with dignity, and keep on loving straight through it. So the greenish blue tablet I settle on delivers a dose of guilt along with its prescribed promised comfort.

People going through a crucible sometimes comfort themselves with the thought, "I have no right to complain, it could be worse," as though the only person on the planet who had a right to moan was Job. Nonsense; yes, it could be worse, and it probably will get worse. There is much that I should and don't know, but I am confident that I know what crippling depression feels like.

In his semi-autobiographical bestseller *Either/Or*, Kierkegaard sighs, "My depression is the most faithful mistress I have known—no wonder, then, that I return the love." Ditto. My depression has certainly been faithful to me, faithfully beclouded many joys and, in the process, placed a subtle shroud over my family, sometimes voiced by my children in a quiet "What's up with Dad today?"

Of all the goods that I have allowed the teeth of the black dog to tear from me, none has been more precious than my sense of agency. Maybe it had something to do with all the medications I shot down my gullet, but over the years I lost confidence in my willpower, in my ability to change, in my ability to cope with moods and situations without a pill in the pocket. Occasionally, I have been granted the reprieve of a good night's sleep. Before breakfast I might resolve something like regularly reading the Bible or maybe going to the meditation center, but by dusk my morning intentions are in the rearview mirror. In a form of gallows humor, I regularly joke about a morning self and an evening self. The morning self had one plan, the weary, cynical evening self another—instead of prayers and meditation, maybe a couple of pints and some superficial have-to-watch series on the appropriately named boob tube. A Buddhist teacher once told me that all the self-improvement regimes were tinged with violence since they all presupposed a lack of self-acceptance, that you are not good enough to start with. My evening self liked that idea.

Then I encountered something in Kierkegaard that shed fresh light on my darkling inner life, namely, a long-lost distinction between depression and despair, between a psychological and a spiritual disorder. Though many Americans blithely talk about being spiritual, they seldom if ever distinguish between psychological and spiritual maladies. These days, confide to someone that you are in despair and he or she will surely suggest that you seek out professional help for your depression. While despair used to be classified as one of the seven deadly sins, it has now been folded into the concept of clinical depression. If Kierkegaard were on Facebook, he would surely complain that we who have listened to Prozac have grown deaf to the difference between a disruption in the way we feel and a sickness in our very being.

Kierkegaard was a late child of Romanticism, which stressed our connection to nature and the belief that the secrets of the universe were conveyed, feelingly, in the emotions. Johann Wolfgang von Goethe (1749–1832) and his immensely influential *Sorrows of Young Werther* were paradigmatic of this anti-rationalist movement. Going back to Aristotle, melancholy was regarded as the affliction of geniuses, perhaps belying the fact that great art and insights into human nature are often born of intense suffering. In *Either/Or*, Kierkegaard begins with a quintessential expression of Romanticism:

> What is a poet? An unhappy person who conceals profound anguish in his heart but whose lips are so formed that as sighs and cries pass over them they sound like beautiful music. It is with him as with the poor wretches in Phalaris's bronze bull, who were slowly tortured over a slow fire; their screams could not reach the tyrant's ears to terrify him; to him they sounded like sweet music.[2]

Like the present era, the age of Romanticism was one in which melancholy was the disease du jour. Kierkegaard was

If Kierkegaard were on Facebook, he would surely complain that we who have listened to Prozac have grown
deaf to the difference between a disruption in the way
we feel and a sickness in our very being.

no exception. Take for instance, this deep sigh emitted in
his journals in 1836:

> I have just returned from a party of which I was the
> life and soul; witticisms poured from my lips, every-
> body laughed and admired me—but I left, yes, the
> dash should be as long as the radii of the earth's orbit—
>
> ———and wanted to shoot myself.[3]

And this, another of scores of such plaintive entries:

> From the very beginning I have been in the power of
> a congenital mental depression. If I had been brought
> up in a more ordinary way—well, it stands to reason
> that I then would hardly have become so melancholy.[4]

Make no mistake about it, Kierkegaard was familiar with
the sorrowful feelings that so many of us drag to the clinic.
Søren's pietistic father, Michael Pedersen Kierkegaard, was

fifty-seven when Søren was born. Kierkegaard was profoundly attached to the brilliant but quietly stern old man who would cast a pall over his son's life. Kierkegaard remarked, "An old man, who himself suffered exceedingly from melancholy, has a son in his old age, who inherits all this melancholy." In another strange morsel, Kierkegaard observes that his father ruined his prospects for happiness, but thanks him for preparing him for a life of faith.

In Kierkegaard's Danish, there are two terms used for depression: *melancholi* and *tungsindighed*. The latter underscores the physical resonances of depression and literally translates into something like "heavy-mindedness." Kierkegaard was a perspicacious student of moods and their significance. Recall Kierkegaard's analysis of anxiety. While fear has a distinct object, anxiety does not; it comes with a veritable shooting gallery of objects. Depression, then, is a first cousin of angst.

In the second volume of *Either/Or*, one of Kierkegaard's pseudonyms observes:

> There is something unexplainable in depression [*Tungsind*]. A person with a sorrow or a worry knows why he sorrows or worries. If a depressed person is asked what the reason is, what it is that weighs [*tynge*] on him, he will answer: I do not know; I cannot explain it. Therein lies the limitlessness of depression.[5]

And so, even in our own time, depression has been aptly described as the "inexplicable sadness."

To listen to Kierkegaard, our moods run the gamut from giddiness to depression. Distinguishing between shades of gloom and doom is a difficult and inexact art. To reiterate, there is a sense in which our inner experiences are socially constructed. It has, for instance, been argued that for lack of leisure time, no one talked about being bored until the eighteenth century. After the Second World War, one would hear that so-and-so had a nervous breakdown, but nothing about "panic attacks." Always in flux, the way we pick out and label our experiences shapes our experiences.

And yet, as Robert Burton's 1621 classic *The Anatomy of Melancholy* attests, even as accounts of the etiology of depression continue to evolve, there is an age-old consistency in the depictions of the experience spanning back millennia. In other words, it would not have been a stretch for Kierkegaard to identify with the same self-tortured, stuck, hopeless feeling we so commonly moan about today. However, for Kierkegaard depression does not necessarily imply despair, nor does being in despair necessarily imply depression.

Today, scarcely anyone believes that a person can be of troubled mind and healthy spirit; and it is hard to fathom the idea that someone who is all smiles might be a case of despair. With physical health, it is, however, conceivable that someone might believe she is in superb condition and yet be on death's door. I know a bodybuilder who made just this fatal misjudgment. In order to assess health, you need to possess the right conception of health; likewise, with spiritual health. While we can't be mistaken about whether or not we are feeling pleasure or pain, we can, says Kierkegaard, be mistaken about our spiritual fettle. On his account, you can feel as though you are in a very good place when you are actually in the depths of despair. You can't be happy and be depressed, but, to paraphrase the author of *The Sickness unto Death*, happiness is despair's greatest hiding place, which is to say that happiness is not the right touchstone for spiritual well-being.[6]

There is a sense in which the Lutheran Kierkegaard was the Luther of the Lutheran tradition. But for all their differences, like Luther, Kierkegaard was a true believer that there are two kingdoms, two realms of reality, the spiritual and the earthly. Apropos of these two realms, Kierkegaard frequently points out that two people might be using the same word, one in an earthly sense and the other in a spiritual. In these instances, it seems as though the interlocutors are referring to the same phenomenon when they are actually talking past one another. The worldly understanding of despair calls to mind a distinctly *desperate* feeling. As Kierkegaard scholar Vincent McCarthy has observed, in English, "despair" draws from the French *désespoir*, indicating the negation of *espoir* (hope).[7] However, spiritually understood, despair is something altogether different from the feeling of hopelessness. In fact, to take a cue from Kierkegaard, it is not connected with any specific feeling; instead, despair is a sickness of the self, manifested along a continuum from being ignorant of having a self to refusing to become yourself. How can someone be ignorant of having or being a self? Kierkegaard addresses the question at book length in his masterpiece, *The Sickness unto Death*.

Almost as a challenge to rebuff the less than serious reader, Kierkegaard begins this work, published in 1849, with a passage that we have already visited and will return to in almost every chapter, because these two sentences encapsulate the fact that we are self-relating creatures. Again,

> A human being is spirit. But what is spirit? Spirit is the self. But what is the self? The self is a relation that relates itself to itself or is the relation's relating itself to itself in the relation.

For those who do not immediately pitch the book across the room, Kierkegaard continues, "A human being is a synthesis of the infinite and the finite, of the temporal and the eternal, of freedom and necessity."[8] It has nothing to do with feeling down; at first glance despair occurs when there is an imbalance in this synthesis.

After taking a stab at a definition, Kierkegaard presents a veritable portrait gallery of the forms that despair takes. Too much of the expansive factor, of infinitude, and you have the dreamer who cannot make anything concrete. Too much of the limiting element yields the narrow-minded individual who cannot think of anything more serious in life than bottom lines and spreadsheets.

The primary symptom of despair is a conscious or unconscious desire to get rid of the self. More often than not, this desire takes the form of flat-out wanting to be someone else. In a telling passage, Kierkegaard writes:

> An individual in despair despairs over *something*. So it seems for a moment, but only for a moment; in the same moment the true despair or despair in its true form shows itself. In despairing over *something*, he really despaired over *himself*, and now he wants to be rid of himself. For example, when the ambitious man whose slogan is "Either Caesar or nothing" does not get to be Caesar, he despairs over it . . . precisely because he did not get to be Caesar, he now cannot bear to be himself.[9]

Childish as it now seems, when I was a young man, I lived by the creed "The NFL or nothing." During my playing days, the Vietnam War was in full flame. I could discuss the issue, but regrettably I didn't care half as much about my brothers and sisters in arms as I did about my gridiron ambitions. I didn't want to be myself unless it was a self on some NFL roster. It all came crashing down quickly in college, and when it did, I felt invisible, unmanned. If asked, I would have groaned that I was despairing *over* the loss of football. On Kierkegaard's reckoning, it would have been more precise to say that I was despairing over having to be myself without my identity as a football player. I wanted to be rid of myself, and there were many nights when I nearly managed to do just that.

Americans seem to live in the future. We incessantly spout pieties about having some dreamed-up vision of the self that we desperately want to realize. Young people who lack such a vision are looked upon askance. It could be making a million by thirty or becoming a surgeon or maybe becoming the next JAY-Z or Ryan Gosling. Apparently, the present only acquires significance for us as a stepping stone to the pedestal of some triumphant future moment.

But suppose you publish that novel to rave reviews or land that role in Hollywood. Suppose you realize that ideal self. Suppose you become Caesar? You are, of course, in seventh heaven, "a state," Kierkegaard remarks, "that is in another sense just as despairing"; just as despairing as failing to realize your dream.

In *The Sickness unto Death*, Kierkegaard envisioned three sorts of selves. First there is the concrete self. Permit me to introduce him or her. As a professor of more than twenty years, I have encountered myriad students completely absorbed with the *ambition* of becoming a doctor. For some, their every move in life seems directed at attaining this goal. In this case, the concrete self might be the senior cramming for MCATs, beefing up her résumé by tutoring struggling high school students, and becoming certified as an EMT. The ideal, or second, self, the self that she fervently wants to become, is someone wearing a stethoscope around her neck, that is, a doctor.

But what of the third self? That is the true self, one that is not particularly interesting in and of itself. This self has nothing to do with your station or accomplishments. As Kierkegaard has it, that neglected but most important self would be a self who "rested transparently in God," a self who made the movements of faith and from which a certain repertoire of feeling and behaviors issued forth. For those who roll their eyes in disappointment at such pietistic palaver, you could picture that third self as your moral ideal, as the *sort* of person you aspire to be, of the kind of individual who reminds you of what we are capable of.

Most people who go the extra ten miles never attract public attention. And yet, I recently read of two young Americans working as volunteer medics on the front lines in Mosul. At terrible risk, they were so close to the fierce fighting that none of the NGOs was allowed in the same precincts. These twentysomething buddies were not physicians, only trained medics with scant medical supplies. Still, scores of severely wounded civilians and soldiers were rushed daily to their encampment. I don't know what has become of these brave men. They were a blip in between news cycles, but they surely could have been doing a lot of other things besides imperiling their lives and limbs. Who knows what went on in their heads. Who knows the full story of their motives, but it is easy to imagine this dauntless duo as Samaritans striving to realize something akin to the Kierkegaardian third self.

Kierkegaard suspects that people who fulfill their ideal selves will be inclined to think that they have hit the bull's-eye of life. And why shouldn't they? Maybe you are a big shot CEO whom everyone depends on and no one ever calls to task. In Plato's *Apology*, Socrates recalls that when he was looking for proof that he, Socrates, was not the wisest person in Athens, he went to the craftsmen, who, unlike the politicians, actually knew something. But because of their lack of wisdom, the craftsmen imagined that because they were good at making harnesses or perhaps money, they knew everything. I suppose the same hubristic mentality is a temptation for people who realize their ideal selves. They thank God for their success, perhaps secretly thinking that at some level God looked favorably upon them for a reason, because they deserved it. In contrast, those of us who bumble, who fall on hard times, who are depressed might be forced to some degree of self-reflection. With a dash of awareness, we might even be moved to ask ourselves, How could I be so caught up in my ambitions as to feel I was worthless unless I made it to the NFL? Or again, for someone going through a breakup, How could my sense of self be so tenuous that I feel as though I don't have any purpose on this earth unless I am partnered up with so-and-so? On this analysis, spiritually speaking, fortunate sons and daughters might not be so fortunate. Remember, "happiness is despair's greatest hiding place." And the seventh heaven of success can be the dung heap of despair when you forget what you are actually here for.

Contrarily, the depressive slogging through the bleakest of times need not to be in despair. Kierkegaard recognized that he was a depressive, but he also judged that he was in decent spiritual health. In 1846, he wrote a note to himself:

> I am in the profoundest sense an unhappy individuality, riveted from the beginning to one or another suffering bordering on madness, a suffering which must have its deepest basis in a misrelation between my mind and body, for (and this is the remarkable thing as well as my infinite encouragement) it has no relation to my spirit.[10]

Depression metastasizes into despair by virtue of the way the depressed individual relates herself to her depression. When a person is ill and can't concentrate on anything but his discomfort and pain, we say that he is in poor spirits. When a sick and hobbled individual can escape her own agony to care for others, we say she is in good spirits, not a good mood, but good spirits. It is no different with psychic pain, with depression. Kierkegaard wants us to understand that while we might not have much choice in how we feel at a given time, we have control over and responsibility for the way we relate ourselves to those feelings. Having sway over our emotions requires an awareness of those emotions, which is not always easy.

Be it sadness, jealousy, or rage, most of us find it hard to acknowledge Gorgon-like feelings, especially those of the sort that make us feel out of control or less than virtuous. Today we are invited to believe that many of our negative emotions are illnesses to be treated. In their *The Loss of Sadness*, authors Allan Horwitz and Jerome Wakefield contend that with the medicalization of just about everything, we have arrived at treating ordinary sadness as if it were a depressive illness. These days, when a loved one is dying, it is not unusual for a physician to suggest a round of prophylactic antidepressants to close family members. We have come to treat grief, a sign of the invisible ties that bind us to one another, as a symptom. Psychologically speaking, being

---

While we might not have much choice in how we feel at a given time, we have control over and responsibility for the way we relate ourselves to those feelings. Having sway over our emotions requires an awareness of those emotions, which is not always easy.

---

invited to believe that intensely negative emotions lasting more than a week are psychologically symptomatic does not exactly motivate a person to try to sit with and process those emotions. Take it from someone who has sometimes sought the "peace that surpasses all understanding" in bottles of various kinds. Taken to a fundamentalist level, the medical model of mental illness does not instill confidence that I can be a caring human being when the all-encompassing numbness is wrapping its cold arms around me. Kierkegaard attests that depression develops into despair—into a spiritual malady—only when we let ourselves be defined by our depression and, in our hopelessness, toss in the towel on our moral and spiritual aspirations. That surrender is despair, not depression.

In 1845, Kierkegaard published *Three Discourses on Imagined Situations*, which celebrated the sacral subjects of confession, marriage, and death. In his discourse "At a Graveside," what might be his all-time most powerful spate of pages, Kierkegaard trumpets *alvorlighed*, which has been translated into English as "seriousness" or "earnestness." These terms are difficult for modern readers to appreciate, let alone relate to. Good character we can grasp, but earnestness does not ring a bell. Nonetheless, in this text, becoming earnest looms as more important than happiness, the universally recognized goal of life. Yes, happiness might require certain virtues. Still, it is very much a matter of fortune—being born at the right time, in the right place, to the right family, with the right talents. All these contingencies redouble our prospects for leading a meaningful and pleasant life. But whatever earnestness is, it is not like happiness, and fortune, the lottery of life, has nothing to do with it.

Kierkegaard attests that depression develops into despair—into a spiritual malady—only when we let ourselves be defined by our depression and, in our hopelessness, toss in the towel on our moral and spiritual aspirations. That surrender is despair, not depression.

In depression, we are removed from the present, masticating past missteps and anticipating the horrors in the offing. Much like faith, earnestness is "movement of the spirit" that is not easily detected by the naked eye. "At a Graveside" portrays the earnest individual as someone who is profoundly aware that the kite string of his life could be cut at any moment. That awareness prods him to recollect the eternal while he is in time. By "recollect" Kierkegaard means that the earnest person does not just "remember" God, he makes himself contemporary with the eternal. Though his life is measured by the hourglass, he sustains a connection with that which is outside of time and unchanging. Again, earnestness is for us a remote concept, but while engaged in life, such an individual would see the buzz of earthly existence for what it is, one addicted to comparisons: who has the bigger salary, the more important job, the fancier plot in the cemetery? Just the other day, I was beside myself, knocked out of all tenderness, because a friend received an endowed professorship. "I'm so happy for you," I effused, but not really. Jealousy is one of the thorny bushes on life's way, and comparisons are the loam of jealousy. The earnest person is made of flesh and blood, and as such will naturally experience those green feelings, but ultimately he will not measure himself or his life by comparisons with others. His measuring stick is one of becoming that third self.

At one point in "At a Graveside," Kierkegaard's nondescript spiritual paragon feels shaken and despondent by the thought of death. Instead of permitting this innervating feeling to gain the upper hand, he reminds himself, "My soul is in a mood, and if it continues this way, then there is in it a hostility toward me that can gain dominion."[11] And should that hostile mood triumph, he realizes, there is an all-too-human tendency to take the trapdoor and try to sink through the bottom of the depression. I have often heard floundering friends and even the bearded guy in the mirror protest, "I need to hit bottom before I can begin to get better." Cognizant that there is no bottom, that we can always sink deeper, Kierkegaard writes, "It is the cowardly craving of depression to want to become dizzy in the emptiness and to seek the final diversion in this dizziness."[12] The earnest individual tells him- or herself, "Wake up, don't allow depression to develop into despair."

Depression is not despair, but depression can certainly lay down the tracks to despair. Circumventing despair requires keeping a third eye on your inner life. It requires keeping a part of yourself outside the inner morass of long-standing bilious moods. The desert monks of the third century wrote of the dangers of *acedia*, the noonday demon, a state marked by agitation, weakness, lack of motivation, and above all indifference to the good and to oneself. Indeed, the roots of the Greek for acedia are *a* (without) *keidos* (care). The cure often prescribed for acedia was none other than manual labor, which seems like something my high school principal would have come up with.

Depression is not despair, but depression can certainly lay down the tracks to despair. Circumventing despair requires keeping a third eye on your inner life. It requires keeping a part of yourself outside the inner morass of bilious moods.

For some, however, antidepressants can also provide a life preserver. In his honest and insightful *A Hell of Mercy*, Tim Farrington writes of suffering from a withering decades-long depression. Farrington seeks to differentiate plain old pathological depression from St. John of the Cross's "dark night of the soul," which dissolves the ego to leave an opening for God. He makes rigorous and consistent efforts at everything from Zen and yoga to living in a monastery. After his mother's death, Farrington is hospitalized and, over time, hammered into a hopeless and passive acceptance of the world, an acceptance that seems to closely resemble acedia. One day, an old and chronically depressed friend visits. Much more upbeat than ever before, she reports having been on a course of antidepressants and burbles, "It's changed my life . . . I wish I'd started twenty years ago." After having resisted antidepressants for years, Farrington agrees to give them a try. His wife is so relieved that she sobs with joy. Farrington starts on a cycle of Effexor, and almost miraculously feels as though he were born again. He writes:

> A good proportion of the side effects duly occurred, but about a week after I started on the drug I was driving home one afternoon with a bag of groceries and a pack of cigarettes and I noticed how beautiful the winter trees were in the crystalline February light. That got my attention all right. It seemed like forever since I had noticed any trees.[13]

Judging from the coda to Farrington's chronicle, the magic potion continues to do its work. One might expect that Farrington would regret all the desert-like experiences he has undergone before the coming of his pharmacological savior. But instead, he writes, "It is in that surrender, in the embrace of our own perceived futility that real freedom comes."[14]

The ultimate truth, the one most of us can't brook, is that of our total vulnerability and dependence on God. But Farrington's point is that lifelong suffering and a completely joyless existence are not prerequisites for achieving this understanding. After all, Jesus himself wanted to pass the cup. You don't have to be on the rack your entire life to fathom that you should stop grasping for control.

In contrast, Kierkegaard was adamant about keeping the thorn in his side from beginning to end. In fact, he insisted that the one thing he never prayed for was for the "thorn in his flesh" to be removed, and that thorn was his depression. But his faithfulness to his mistress melancholy was idiosyncratic. A thinker of his preternatural powers could have easily floated off into the empyrean, could easily have become intoxicated with his otherworldly abilities; however, his ever-present melancholy helped remind him that his books about faith and earnestness did not in any way ensure that he was a faithful and earnest individual.

Kierkegaard also felt blessed by his depression because it helped keep him alert to the fact that "we are always wrong before God," that we are sinners. And Kierkegaard was insistent that we are more in need of a revelation to understand that we are sinners than to believe we have been saved. There may be something uplifting in Kierkegaard's grateful attitude toward his saturnine nature, but the message that we are always in the wrong is one that depressives are inclined to assimilate into their cruel instruments of self-torture. Realistic guilt is one thing, neurotic self-immolation another—and it is in the latter that depressives excel. But when it is prevented from ransacking our existence, depression can be the vehicle of a kind of wisdom.

Nietzsche's most famous adage is "What doesn't kill you makes you stronger." This, of course, is far from a universal truth since what comes close to killing us often weakens our spirit, then slowly kills us. Still, depression kept at bay can augment our ability to empathize with those feeling broken and without purpose. A friend of mine with three children lost his wife and developed throat cancer in the same year. A few years back, I had a student who was quiet and always sat in the rear of the classroom; one afternoon, he confided that it was hard to concentrate because both of his parents had died separately in a nine-month period. Naturally, he felt so abysmally sad and lonely that he could not keep his mind on anything. There are millions of refugees floating around the globe, often despised and looked down upon by the countries in which they find a tent and temporary anchorage. Not to diminish their agony, but, at a certain pitch, pain and misfortune make refugees of us all. I had another student whose eleven-year-old sister died of leukemia. Likening grief to a modern form of leprosy, he wrote a touching opinion piece in which he maintained that people don't know how to address the bereaved and so they, or we, avoid the stricken as though we might catch something.[15] If loving our neighbors as ourselves is the second most important task in life, then perhaps that lingering sad and anxious feeling that might come out of nowhere can soften our hearts and help us accomplish that less-than-glamorous fundamental task.

Can you be an existentialist and a Tibetan monk? I don't see why not. Tibetan Buddhist monk Pema Chödrön knows what it is to be under the thumb of feeling worthless. It may ring naive, but Chödrön suggests that when under siege, we should gently battle the tempting and benumbing thought that the world is crazy and there is nothing we can do. Instead, we should whisper to ourselves that we have millions of cellmates all over the world enduring the same or similar funk. It is easy to say but hard to appropriate the notion that depression should help us to fathom our vulnerability and dependence on one another.

A frequent chord in this book is that our feelings are one thing, and the way we relate to our feelings another. Chödrön teaches that when the feeling of worthlessness crashes our gates, we should not think that we have been singled out. Instead of feeling isolated in a cage of our suffering, we should pry open our black-and-blue hearts and send out love and compassion to all our self-torturing brothers and sisters; in a secular sense, that would be depression without despair.

CHAPTER
3

DEATH

One frozen February night, when I was in my early twenties, I was driving back to New Jersey with a friend, from where I don't remember, and singing along with the Stones' raucous "Dancing with Mr. D." We decided to stop at Niagara Falls. It was well past midnight and must have been about ten below. A chain-link fence descended an icy decline to the lip of the falls. Whooping and laughing, I crept hand over hand along the fence, down to the edge, and hung out over the thunderously gushing waters. One slip and it would have been adios. But no worries; back then I enjoyed pulling on the whiskers of the grim reaper. I felt immortal.

Kierkegaard, Tolstoy, Camus, Heidegger, and other existentialists were always walking back and forth over their graves, always thinking about the meaning of death in life. When I teach existentialism, there is no topic that my eighteen- and nineteen-year-olds warm to more than death. Most of them have seen thousands upon thousands of people blown to bits or take bullets to the chest on screens and in video games, but most of them have yet to sit on the couch with death, close enough to smell its breath. They have not been bedside it in the ICU with those green lights bleeping, feeding a loved one ice chips as he fades out of existence. My students like to have pillow fights with death, just as I did when I was their age. Who knows, maybe it was because I felt dead inside, but even when I was in my midthirties, I wrote about death for my dissertation. Looking back, I think that even then, as a mature man and father, I was just jousting with the idea, although now I wasn't hanging out over Niagara Falls; it was an intellectual game.

Things have changed; now that I have sat by my father, who with that oxygen mask and grotesquely distorted blown-up face, was being blasted by cancer out of the world he could never get right with; now that I have listened to my mother's death rattle for a week before feeling her shins go cold and death creep up her body like a force; now that I have shuffled my feet and rubbed my palms together, waiting to find out the results of my wife's mastectomy and whether or not the cancer had spread; now that I have had a stent in my heart and am in my seventh decade, I am not so much inclined to want to play hide-and-seek with "Mr. D."

Though we don't know the number, we know our days are numbered, or at least the rational part of us knows this. Death is the certain uncertainty that frames our lives. Certain it will happen; uncertain when.

These days, thanatology has become an area of academic specialization. There is an emerging science of how to die and deal with death, as if by turning death into a research subject we could control it. Often outlining the stages of grief and with mantras about "letting go," psychologists and other lifestyle engineers have produced a mountainous literature on death and dying.

Psychology aside, there is a long and august tradition in philosophy of meditating on death. Medieval scholars kept a skull on their desk to remind them that it is dust to dust. Socrates believed that philosophy, rather than an art of living, was a practice in dying, a lifelong practice in separating yourself from the senses and emotions that he thought obscured the sidereal light of reason. Socrates was the patron saint of the Stoics. Buddhist-like, the Stoics took ataraxy, or peace of mind, to be of supreme value. They were convinced that there is no greater threat to inner tranquility than the dread of death. Marcus Aurelius and the company of Stoics believed that the fear of extinction made slaves of us all.

They argued that as long as we are willing to do anything to remain aboveground, we might as well be in shackles. For the Stoics, death carried with it the positive aspect of escaping life when and if it became unbearable. As they were wont to say, "The door is always open." I don't think the Stoics would have been big fans of suicide hotlines. For them, there were fates much worse than death—like becoming a reprobate. If a Nazi-like regime takes control and you don't believe that you can lead a virtuous and tranquil life with such brigands in power, then take your leave, just as Cato, Seneca, and many other Stoics did. And yet, for all their machinations on how to wrangle with death, the Stoics did not discern any great lessons from death.

In the late nineteenth century, Schopenhauer wrote of death as though it were the dividing line of consciousness:

> The cheerfulness and vivacity of youth are partly due to the fact that when we are ascending the hill of life, death is not visible: it lies down at the bottom of the other side. But once we crossed the top of the hill, death comes in view—death, which, until then, was only known by hearsay. . . . A grave seriousness now takes the place of the early extravagance of spirit; and the change is noticeable even in the expression of a man's face. . . . For towards the close of life, every day gives us the same kind of sensation as the criminal experiences at every step on his way to be tried.[1]

Schopenhauer's observations hit the mark. Most of us feel invincible in our youth; then, when we discover that lump on our neck and we can make out the edge of our existence, we grow fearful and forlorn. A depth psychologist whom Freud carefully studied, Schopenhauer espoused the view that the highest achievement in life is to overcome the will to live. Still, like the Stoics, he did not expect any special wisdom to come from pondering his demise. Tolstoy, in contrast, did take instruction from his own mortality.

An officer in the Crimean War, Tolstoy was no stranger to death and carnage. Still, when he was in his early thirties and his beloved brother Nikolai died, the Russian giant sank into a withering depression. Tolstoy was known for his preternatural physical strength and energy. He labored long hours in the field and, at the same time, wrote the likes of *War and Peace* and *Anna Karenina*. And yet, for a couple of years after Nikolai's death, the strong man was blanketed in depression. He could not absorb the preposterous fact that we are thrown into an existence in which we claw to survive, in which we bind ourselves to others so intimately that it feels as though our hearts were outside ourselves, only to have a few molecules move one way or the other and—*poof*—we pop like a balloon and all is over. Nicodemus stealthily came to Jesus at night. Jesus knew what he was seeking—life everlasting. In his *Confessions*, Tolstoy, another Nicodemus, sighed, "I cannot now help seeing day and night going round and bringing me to death. That is all I see, for that alone is true. All else is false."

Freud, who famously taught that belief in God was a projection of a childish wish for protection, would chuckle at Tolstoy's conversion to Christianity, but the devout Tolstoy came to believe in Christ because he believed that only Christ promised victory over death.

Downcast as he was, Tolstoy managed to compose *The Death of Ivan Ilych*. This lambent little book masterfully portrays bourgeois society's nervousness, alienation, self-estrangement, and moribund spiritual life. Tolstoy was a close reader of the French mathematician and philosopher Blaise Pascal (1623–1662), who remarked that if human beings could only learn to sit still with themselves, there would be peace on earth. Tolstoy agreed with Pascal, but in *The Death of Ivan Ilych* he connects the craving for diversion and our alienation from one another with our unspoken terror of death.

Tolstoy's protagonist, Ivan Ilych, savors a life that, despite a few bumps, seems to all, including himself, to be going swimmingly. Throughout the novella, Tolstoy describes the promotions and acquisitions that are supposed to make the barrister feel as though everything was snug and safe in life. For the escalator class, new homes were essential markers of blessedness. After some challenging times, Ivan enjoys a stroke of luck and is appointed a judge. Naturally, he builds a fancy new home.

One afternoon, while hanging curtains, the judge takes a tumble and slams his side. A few days later, a mysterious and painful affliction develops. The pain, which centers near his kidney, comes and goes, then gradually moves in for good. Day by day, Ivan starts to wither away. He consults with renowned doctors, but no one can make a diagnosis and none of the treatments provide any lasting relief. Like a bright winter sunlight sweeping across a hardwood floor, there are moments of respite and hope that come and go. Gradually, however, Ivan grasps that he is pregnant with his own death. At one point, he overhears his brother-in-law lecturing Praskovya, Ivan's wife, that Ivan is dying. And yet no one, not even the doctors, acknowledges that he is near the end. Ivan is as isolated as someone stricken with the plague. Laden with horror, sadness, and fury at the world and God, the poor man has no one to turn to and unburden himself: not his frivolous helpmate, not his equally superficial daughter, not his bridge-partner friends. At one point when he is in his bedroom listening to the chatter from a soiree that his wife has arranged, Ivan fumes, "Death. Yes, death. And none of them know or wish to know it, and they have no pity for me."

The sole person able to empathize with the dying man is his servant Gerasim. As his pain crescendos, Ivan finds comfort when Gerasim takes Ivan's legs and rests them on his broad shoulders. Late one night, as Ivan was sending the young man away and expressing his gratitude for his servant's generous efforts, Gerasim offhandedly gave voice to the inconvenient truth that Ivan was dying, saying, "We shall all of us die, so why should I grudge a little trouble."

It is obtuse to reduce a novel or poem to a message fit for an index or Hallmark card, as though if Tolstoy were *really* intelligent he would have stopped teasing us and just straightforwardly informed us *what his novel meant.* Yet the Tolstoy of *Ivan Ilych* wanted his readers to understand that, with its lack of authenticity and brotherly love, modern life is spiritual death.

As Ivan is slowly forced to crawl into the womb of his death, the chapters in *The Death of Ivan Ilych* grow shorter and shorter. Up until the very end, Ivan expresses his chagrin and perplexity at the fact that someone like him—someone who had done everything "right," everything he was supposed to do—could be doomed to this dreadful fate of annihilation. It didn't seem fair. But in his agony and throes of his death anxiety, the truth wafts up. Dying teaches Ivan the humanity that living could not. He begins to comprehend that he and his social set are a cast of soulless careerists whose only worries are their income, comfort level, and social standing.

The light of death illuminates the fact that he and his wife have long been estranged. As he lay dying, Praskovya approaches Ivan "with undried tears on her nose and cheek and a despairing look on her face." In his final moments,

Ivan escapes the lifelong orbit of his all-consuming selfishness. He thinks, "Yes, I am making them wretched." And then, "'it will be better for them when I die.' He wished to say this but had not the strength. . . . With a look at his wife he indicated his son and said: 'Take him away . . . sorry for him . . . sorry for you, too. . . .' He tried to add, 'Forgive me,' but said 'forgo' and waved his hand, knowing that He whose understanding mattered would understand."

The awareness of death that everyone was eager to repress was alone capable of producing the intimacy with his family that Ivan was not even aware that he longed for. It was only when the hourglass had run out that Ivan understood this, but maybe that was enough.

Tolstoy was friends with a Dane living in Russia, who was a fervent fan of his countryman Kierkegaard. Tolstoy's Danish friend enjoyed translating fragments from Kierkegaard's *Enten/Eller* (*Either/Or*) and reading them aloud to Tolstoy in Russian. Although Tolstoy was less than impressed with the disparate snippets, Tolstoy and Kierkegaard were kindred spirits. Both of them recognized the collision between reason and faith. Both underscored the individual's relation to God over the individual's relation to the ecumenical institutions mediating our relationship with God. Both accentuated action over creedal assent. Finally, Kierkegaard no less than Tolstoy, and for some of the same moral reasons, urged us to think death over, or rather to think our *own* death over.

Most of the writers classified as existentialists are critical of the aspiration to ponder the world and history from a perspectiveless perspective. They were doubting Thomases about the desirability of striving to think about the meaning of our lives from a passionless, objective standpoint. It was, they believed, an Enlightenment fantasy to imagine that we could have a disinterested understanding of matters that should be of infinite interest, most pressingly ethics and religion, as though we could or should try to answer the question of what kind of person we should strive to be through some cool and collected rational process. Whether or not to tether your life to God or brush the divinity issue off as nonsense is a resolve that partially forms what kind of person you will be. To respond to existential choice, as though you were a third party to yourself akin to an impartial judge in court, would, from a Kierkegaardian vantage point, be a contortion of what it means to be human.

As noted above, Kierkegaard prodded us to think about life from a first-person, inside-out vantage point. On his reckoning, philosophers from Plato to Hegel in their excogitations were guilty of living in theory, of "forgetting their existence." Emphatic that death, like anxiety, has lessons for us, Kierkegaard warns that we must be willing to appropriate those lessons personally and passionately. In his philosophical magnum opus, *The Concluding Unscientific Postscript*, Kierkegaard deploys the example of death to highlight the difference between objective facts and the

meaning of those facts, or again, between a general, imper-
sonal knowledge and a personal understanding. He writes:

> For example, *what it means to die*. On that topic, I
> know what people ordinarily know: that if I swallow
> a dose of sulfuric acid I will die, likewise by drowning
> myself or sleeping in coal gas etc. I know that Napoleon
> always carried poison with him, that Shakespeare's
> Juliet took it; that the Stoics regarded suicide as a cou-
> rageous act and others regard it as cowardice, . . . I
> know the tragic hero dies in the fifth act. . . . I know
> that the poet interprets death in a variety of moods.[2]

The Danish firebrand continues his catena of objective
certainties, but then, in one dash of his pen, puts the problem
in our inbox, "However; despite this almost extraordinary
knowledge or proficiency of knowledge, I am by no means
able to regard death as something I have understood."

Kierkegaard prodded us to think about life from a first-
person, inside-out vantage point.

I can know all sorts of general truths about death and
still fail to understand what it means that I shall die. Again,
objective facts and abstract theories are one thing; however,

what those facts and theories personally *mean* to me are something else again. Personal meaning is the bull's-eye of existentialist investigation; in this case, it helps answer the "What does it mean to me that I will die?"

In the previously cited "At a Graveside," Kierkegaard urges us to put a figurative skull on our desks. In this discourse, he nods to the apparent contradiction of an existing individual thinking of him- or herself as nonexistent; nevertheless, Kierkegaard assures us that with a little imagination and courage, we can unite these immiscibles. We can think about ourselves and our death.

Imagining your own death is a taxing exercise. Kierkegaard observed that when it came to keeping company with this idea, our thoughts frequently miss the mark, tending instead toward being projections of current psychological states and, in that sense, of being either too heavy- or light-minded, too frivolous or depressive. Whether it be ghoulish or giddy fantasies, the idea of our own death easily becomes a kind of inkblot test in which we expose something deep about our life perspective, rather than actually confronting the fact that there comes a time when there is no more time, when all is over.

Many of the mistaken and misleading ways we have of thinking about our own demise are cataloged in "At a Graveside." It is, for instance, common to hear death described as a sleep. But Kierkegaard jabs, "Look at the one who is sleeping in death; he is not flushed like a child in sleep;

he is not gathering new strength . . . the dream is not paying him a visit in friendliness the way it visits the old man in his sleep!"[3]

Then there is the notion of death as the great equalizer. Maybe the maid who has been cleaning hotel rooms at the Ritz for the pampered class for twenty years is excoriated by a guest for failing to replace a sparkling water in the fridge. She grinds her teeth, bites her tongue, and apologizes all the while silently consoling herself with the bitter thought that everyone is an equal in death, the rich no less than the poor will be food for worms. Though not out of cruelty, Kierkegaard would deny her that comfort. "Death's decision," he comments, "is . . . not definable as equality, because the equality consists in annihilation. And pondering this is supposed to be alleviating for the living!"

"Eat, drink, and be merry" is another gambit, which Kierkegaard casts as a hysterical "cowardly clinging to life." Epicurus taught, "Where I am death is not and where death is I am not." Ergo, a rational person does not fear death. On this piece of logical legerdemain, Kierkegaard wryly remarks, "This is the jest by which the cunning contemplator places himself on the outside," and it is "only a jest if he merely contemplates death and not himself in death."

Kierkegaard recognized that when the hard rain starts to fall, many of us tend to curl up and withdraw into a feeling of hopelessness. We play possum. But the psychoanalyst— with religious categories up his sleeves—upbraids the longing for death, as the "cowardly craving of depression to want to become dizzy in the emptiness and to seek the final diversion in this dizziness."

Unlike more rationalist pates, Kierkegaard had a deep appreciation for the significance of moods. In "At a Graveside," Kierkegaard describes moods as a form of internal weather sparked by something external. Dark and light, moods come and go.

An old friend surprised me last week. We tossed back a couple of beers and, for an hour or three, I was immersed in the moment, the way I used to feel like as an athlete when a football was sailing toward me or a left hook in the boxing ring. All my regrets and worries seemed to seep away. The next day, I got a call informing me that another friend who had long suffered from the inexplicable sadness used a pistol to blow the bad thoughts out of his brains. Clouds of all-consuming sadness engulfed me, forked by the idea that life is as absurd as Camus and Cioran painted it. Kierke-gaard, however, warns that the moods that sweep over us, no matter how powerful, are not to be confused with earnest-ness, that is, with a profound, personal concern about the sort of human being we are becoming.

Sometimes it seems as though God were playing tricks. Kierkegaard's name means "churchyard" in Danish. As a young man, Kierkegaard made many trips to the church-yard. Before he was twenty, he had thrown a handful of dirt on the caskets of his mother and four siblings. And yet he insists that witnessing another person's death, even that of your own child, is *"only a mood,"* an infinitely sad one that might buckle your knees, shake you to the core, and perhaps invite you to think that it would be best to jump in the grave yourself. Just the same, the feeling that comes with the news of a loved one's death is still "only a mood" and not the relation to yourself that only an awareness of your own death can inculcate.

Kierkegaard, however, warns that the moods that sweep over us, no matter how powerful, are not to be confused with earnestness, that is, with a profound, personal concern about the sort of human being we are becoming.

"At a Graveside" begins with the plangent words, *Så er det da forbid!* (So it is over!). Fugue-like, the expression "it is over" is repeated a score of times in the score of pages that follow. Kierkegaard writes as though convinced that this mantra is the best caption to capture and focus our minds on death. One day and again, who knows when, all will be over. You won't be able to change a sentence of the story of your life. Maybe a week ago you resolved to be a more attentive and loving husband. As you were driving home from work, a song drifts over the radio, an otherwise sappy pop tune, "You'll never get to heaven if you break my heart." Insight and wisdom can sift in from the strangest places. And for some reason, the song melts your very being so that you are overcome with a feeling of tenderness and newfound appreciation for the woman who is the mother of your children. The resolve hovers that from now until the end of your days, you are going to kiss your wife on the lips every day and remind her of your boundless love. You stop at a red light that seems to be dancing a jig in the gusty wind. You can't wait to traverse those few extra miles home; home, where you will embrace her and trade stories of the day's events, events that no one but you two would be interested in. It is as though this little ditty woke you up to what a divine gift intimacy is. Just then there is a rumbling explosion in your chest that feels as if it is blowing you into the stratosphere where everything looks so small and far away. You slink over; to everyone else, it will seem that your death was instantaneous, but there was a sliver of time. As the death of Ivan Ilych makes plain, a moment can last an eternity, and that second was long enough to anguish over having squandered the opportunity to be the loving spouse you always meant to be.

Today, and in Kierkegaard's time, people long to die in their sleep, that is, to die without experiencing death; if not in their sleep then a quick death, one that affords the least amount of time, the minimal awareness that while life moves on for everyone else, it is over for you.

In his novel *White Noise*, Don DeLillo writes of a pill

that dissolves the fear of death. Would you want to take it? Kierkegaard would never prescribe it, although Nietzsche might have celebrated such a pill. Perhaps Nietzsche would have judged all this intentional thinking about death to be a perverse waste of time. Rieff, a close reader of Nietzsche, once quipped, "You only live once . . . if then." Nietzsche would have counseled—don't be a fool and squander that one life, morosely pondering the end of that life. When you have the auriferous sunlight, bask in it, grow, take risks, be creative, dance above the abyss of your own impending death. Our Danish counselor would have read this Nietzschean attitude to be one of whistling in the dark; worse yet, for him it would amount to missing the point of life, namely, that of becoming a human being in the fullest sense. When we are in danger of forgetting what is most important, Kierkegaard advised that we should "summon the earnest thought of death" and that thought will give retroactive force to our lives.

The author of "At a Graveside" writes, "The merchant is correct in saying that the commodity certainly has its price . . . and when there is scarcity, the merchant profits."

Time is a commodity, a commodity for which we can use our imagination to create a scarcity. Kierkegaard continues, "With the thought of death the earnest person is able to create a scarcity, so that the year and day receive infinite worth."

Paraphrasing Heidegger, William Barrett, the philosopher who helped introduce existentialism to Americans, wrote: "This death, my death, the death that haunts me is the possibility that I shall lose that world. And as such an internal possibility, it pervades my existence now and at every moment. . . . It is the most extreme and absolute possibility, because it cancels all other possibilities." Speaking for both Kierkegaard and Heidegger, Barrett adds, "Yet if we do not turn away in panic, this vision of our radical finitude brings its own liberation."[4]

More than liberation, death resets our priorities. What seemed a matter of indifference before now assumes a new significance. The reset of our priorities might be from the trivial and external to central and enduring life tasks. For instance, now and again I might ask myself, Have I gone out of my way for anyone today? Have I even made an effort to think about someone else's life from their perspective? Or let me be more concrete. As noted, my wife survived breast cancer and has now developed Parkinson's. Though Parkinson's makes her self-conscious and forces her to constantly think about timing her medications, for the most part she handles the disease as though it were just another

---

At the risk of being pedantic, the Kierkegaardian understanding of death might be this: don't be careless with the people you walk through life with. Don't have arguments and leave them unsettled.

bump in the road of life. On the other hand, her illness makes me furious at existence and/or God. Some nights, until her medication kicks in, her tremors are so powerful that the bed shakes. When she is in the middle of a bad bout, she often has to lie still for a while. One night, I was feeling needy and irritated that she could not be close, and I turned on my side away from her, as if to let her know . . . I don't know what. Then the thought finally started ticking, *One night in the not too distant future it will all be over—one of us won't be here.* Then I came to my senses. I turned over and gently stroked her head. That was a reset.

For the devout Kierkegaard, death serves as a prompt to "recollect God." The ever-present awareness of your death should give a fillip to faith. But once again, it is imperative to ask whether or not his insights have any traction for adherents of the "God is dead" gospel. Perhaps we could translate the wisdom that Kierkegaard extracts from death along secular lines. If you don't believe in God, and yet *love* is a god term for you, you might surmise that there is nothing more precious in life than loving relationships. At the risk of being pedantic, the Kierkegaardian understanding of death might be this: don't be careless with the people you walk through life with. Don't have arguments and leave them unsettled.

When I get it through my head that the silent freight train of oblivion is barreling down on me, I might be less likely to be heedless in my relationships, to snarl at someone and not feel any urgency to repair the damage. Decades ago, I had an argument over the phone with my elder brother, Tom, concerning our ailing mother. Nine years older, he had been like a father to me. Sometimes I don't think I would have survived the craziness in the battle zone that was our home without his love and protection. Tom was so deeply internalized that when I brought up my own boys, I could always detect his warm, playful voice in the way I bantered and romped with my young sons. Just the same, after we hung up the phone, we did not converse for a decade. Perhaps some instructions from death would have been a scarecrow to my pride; perhaps it would have prevented such carelessness on my part; perhaps it would have prodded me to drive the five hours to see him and attempt to settle our grievances. Half-consciously, I figured we would make peace someday, but I must have imagined then that nothing disastrous could happen to either one of us. In our case, my mother's death brought the olive branch; we are once again as close as we were before, but both of us profoundly regret those fallow years when we were at the equator of our lives and did not exchange a word, much less an embrace.

There is much to recommend Kierkegaard's counsel on death, and yet I think he neglects one aspect of it—namely, the plain and pure tincture of sadness. Three years ago, I sat with a dying woman in her late eighties. She happened to be a rather well-known evangelical author, and the flock of her admirers expected her to be eager to sit at the right or left hand of the table in the great beyond. She was a kind and honest woman, and while we were alone, I held her bony fingers and asked, "You know you are dying—are you afraid?" She bit her lip, shook her head, and answered, "Not afraid, but sad, very sad because I am going to miss everyone."

Anyone who aspires to think earnestly about death must include the heavyheartedness that comes when the ties that bind break. The devout cross over that chasm with the belief that we will all be hanging out together again in the hereafter. But my octogenarian friend was faithful as could be and she was nevertheless shrouded in sadness. Even Jesus wept over his impending death in Gethsemane. Some will scoff that in death we won't be able to feel the pain of the loss. But it could be gainsaid that conscious or not, the loss of a good thing—a loss of love, the best thing—remains a loss, and then to contemplate the agony of those who will feel your absence as though it were a continent breaking away is enough to make a person shut Kierkegaard's book and push aside all thoughts about the end; unless you believe, as I do, that our capacity to absorb and tolerate the full weight of grief is part of becoming an authentic human being.

CHAPTER
4

AUTHENTICITY

When we talk about the spirit of the times, it is wise to specify where we are calling from. I live in Minnesota on a block where people plan vacations, expect their kids to go to college, attend yoga classes and/or church. It is called "Minnesota Nice." Stop by to give someone a birthday gift and you're likely to receive a thank-you card before you get home. Even North Star residents suspect that Minnesota Nice can conceal Minnesota Ice, that deep down we suspect our good behavior and better manners are often less than authentic.

But what does *authenticity* even mean? And what does it mean to live authentically?

In the fifties and early sixties, television shows idealizing traditional families and suburban life were wildly popular. At the same time, literary characters such as Holden Caulfield and Willy Loman, like Ivan Ilych long before them, hinted at an undercurrent of fear about becoming a cookie cutter of a human being, a crowd person, the kind of individual who was defined by externals.

Among my suburban cohort and students, the once-urgent issue of authenticity seems to have been lost to selfies, social media branding, and managing your profile on LinkedIn and Facebook, as though everyone has become their own unabashed publicist. It is not who you are but who you seem to be! A well-known Generation X author, Chuck Klosterman, remarked, "I honestly believe that people of my generation despise authenticity, mostly because they're all so envious of it."

Today, the piety is "Follow your passions. Do what you love." Everyone is enjoined to have some dream about their life, and you are authentic to the extent that you doggedly pursue that vision as though it were your essence. Accordingly, Paul Gauguin may have been a creep for leaving his family to paint in Tahiti, but he was acting authentically. In his measured defense of an "ethic of authenticity," renowned philosopher Charles Taylor quotes Gail Sheehy's bestseller *Passages: Predictable Crises of Adult Life* as an example of the authenticity/individual self-fulfillment equation. Sheehy homilizes:

You can't take everything with you when you leave on the midlife journey. You are moving away. Away from institutional claims and other people's agenda. Away from external valuations and accreditations. You are moving out of roles and into the self. If I could give everyone a gift for the send-off on this journey, it would be a tent. A tent for tentativeness. The gift of portable roots. . . . For each of us there is an opportunity to emerge reborn, *authentically* unique. . . . The delights of self-discovery are always available.[1]

There are many philosophical theories about authenticity; however, I don't need a theory to recognize that I have spent much of my life sparring with the fear of being inauthentic. Motored by profound insecurities and by sheer dint of the enormous effort that insecurities can mobilize, I made it into precincts both in sports and academia in which I felt like I didn't belong, and sometimes rightly so. One late autumn afternoon in the early 1980s, my authenticity hang-ups burst out of the closet and nearly uprooted my future.

Everyone is enjoined to have some dream about their life, and you are authentic to the extent that you doggedly pursue that vision as though it were your essence.

When Philip Rieff took me under his wing, it felt like a benediction, one that I surely let all my fellow graduate students know about. A figure cast from *Downton Abbey*, Rieff was extremely formal in both dress and manner, sometimes sporting a top hat and monocle. Though he was an intellectual renegade of sorts—not unlike Kierkegaard—Rieff was devout in his belief that decorum was the last wall of defense between the barbarians in- and outside of us. No "ums" or stumblings in his diction; Rieff was hypnotic. He spoke as though he were reading from a book, a very good book. Decades later, he would write a lengthy volume on charisma, a quality he possessed in great measure, and those of us who studied with him felt the full weight of it in his presence.

One afternoon, Rieff instructed me to meet him to discuss a paper I was writing on Freud and Kierkegaard. Nervously, I ambled into his office clad in jeans, a dashiki, and a single gold earring. Rieff took one glance at me and pulled a face as though he had just bitten into a lemon. "Why do you carry yourself and dress like a thug?" Sniggering, he continued, "And why are you wearing that silly earring?" Interestingly enough, he had seen me dressed like this before but was mum. Either he thought my sartorial tendencies were an aberration or more likely he calculated that I was now attached enough to him that he could criticize me without my doing something self-destructive. Jumped by anxiety, I bumbled an inanity along the lines that the earring was a symbol. "A symbol!" Rieff chortled. "Ten years from now everyone in the business school will be wearing one. A symbol of what?" he asked acerbically. "If you think it is a symbol, then you must know something about its history." He quizzed, "What do you know about these earrings?" Flummoxed, I shrugged. After a few moments of screaming silence, Rieff delivered a short history of the earring, explaining that it was common among the peasants where my ancestors had come from in southern Italy.

You should not implicitly trust memoirs, mine included. Try as we might, conversations from years past are always part fiction. In this case, I cannot recall my exact words, but I vaguely remember uttering something to the effect that, even though I was in a doctoral program at an elite university, I intended to stay true to my background. Even today, I occasionally hear sports celebrities take this tack, pledging that just because they signed a seven-figure contract and live in mansions in the exurbs, they have not forgotten their roots. Without blinking, Rieff peered at me through his thick glasses, placed his long, slender fingers on his desk, and said—and this is verbatim—"Mr. Marino, it's time you started identifying up." Much as I stood in awe of the man, I was now an impulse away from leaping up and telling him where he could stick his identification sermon.

In my addled mind, I was trying to remain authentic,

trying to stay true to who I thought I was—maybe some mildly erudite version of a working-class hero. Rieff must have been right that the attachment was secure because something stopped me from the kind of outburst I was given to, one that would have exploded a relationship that molded my life in positive, otherwise-unimaginable directions.

Is the litmus test of authenticity the gap between who we feel we are and who we present ourselves to be? Camus meditated long and hard on authenticity. Meursault, the protagonist of *The Stranger*—arguably Camus's most famous character—commits a senseless murder but, in the end, is sentenced to death largely because he refuses to tell the magistrate and others what they want to hear, namely, that he is sorry. Meursault will murder but he won't divulge feelings he does not have. "Above all," Camus wrote in his *Notebooks*, "in order to be, never try to seem." That advice is easier written than followed.

Is the litmus test of authenticity the gap between who we feel we are and who we present ourselves to be? "Above all," Camus wrote in his *Notebooks*, "in order to be, never try to seem."

When I commenced my career as a boxing writer, I would sometimes carry myself as though my modicum of ring experience as a professional heavyweight sparring partner entitled me to think that I was not *just* a writer but a member of the elite fistic brotherhood. One afternoon, after a long talk, I was walking with Mike Tyson, who addressed me, saying, "Guys like you and me . . ." I suppose I had pulled the charade off, or Iron Mike let me think I had pulled it off, but I immediately felt that body blow of inauthenticity. I had managed to wrap myself in borrowed clothes, and though I did not correct Tyson, I felt like the not-so-great imposter. Camus again: if you want to be authentic, "don't try to seem." But some of us who might not be so at home in our skin will have *to try* "to try not to seem."

Is there, however, more to authenticity than being devoid of pretenses? Is a con artist authentic because she acknowledges her con artist activities? Or is a kind and generous soul who thinks of herself as selfish inauthentic because of the dissonance between her public and perceived selves?

The theme of authenticity is a red thread that runs through existential texts, all the way back to the Romantics and Rousseau. And yet it is not as though there is an "essence" of authenticity; that is, some property that uniquely defines it, as we define a square as a figure with four equal sides. A physicist and philosopher, Dr. Ben Yacobi sincerely states it:

> The concept of "authenticity" is a human construct, and as such it has no reality independent of minds.

> But is authenticity possible, or even desirable? . . . This
> steers us toward an interpretation of the concept of au-
> thenticity as an absolute, but in general the search for
> absolutes is fruitless.[2]

Though Sartre tries, there is no precisely distinguishing between sincerity and authenticity as one might differentiate between tables and chairs; nor is it possible to generate an unambiguous criterion for deciding whether or not we are leading authentic lives. This lack of exactitude applies to all our attempts to parse the ingredients of the inner life.

In *Works of Love*, Kierkegaard wrote, "all human speech . . . about the spiritual is essentially metaphorical speech."[3] You can talk about the movement of the wind in the trees *literally* but not the "movement" of the spirit. With a delicious metaphor, Nietzsche announces, "Truth is a mobile army of metaphors." And we need rich metaphors to daub authenticity.

The philosopher and critic Theodore Adorno groused in his *Jargon of Authenticity* that much of the gauzy language generated by such figures as Kierkegaard and Heidegger is enticing but ultimately empty chatter. It is the kind of talk that gulls a reader into believing there are real issues being discussed when, in fact, the only reality is an illusion conjured by fancy words. Atheists moan about religious mumbo jumbo but Adorno contends that philosophy has its own storehouse of the same in what he derisively terms "the liturgy of intimacy." For Adorno, all the sophisticated chatter about authenticity, about becoming yourself, is grounded in the fallacious assumption that each of us possesses an individual soul-like essence discernible by introspection. Nietzsche might have retorted that originality is the ability "to see something that has no name as yet and hence cannot be mentioned although it stares us all in the face."[4] Such might be the case with authenticity.

To reiterate a common theme, we are relational entities. We exist in relation to ourselves, in relation to others and to our surroundings, and for some of us, we believe or try to trust that we exist in relation to God. Given our relational nature, it is reasonable to think that there are true (authentic) and false (inauthentic) ways of connecting to ourselves and others, where *true* would imply open and honest and *false* would imply dissembling relationships.

A student of Nietzsche, Kierkegaard, and Tolstoy, Heidegger abstains from referring to people in the traditional terms of subjects and objects. Instead, he refers to humans using the neologism *Dasein*, which translates to "being there." Make of this what you will, but for Heidegger a human being is essentially an opening in being itself—an opening in which being questions the meaning of being. Other than humans, there do not seem to be any other creatures entranced by problems such as "What is the meaning of life?"

Or Heidegger's "Why is there something rather than nothing?" As Sartre argues in *Being and Nothingness*, Dasein brings nothingness into being, vis-à-vis the interrogation of our own being.

The phenomenological story in something smaller than a nutshell is this: Dasein is cast into existence with distinct abilities and in a nexus of culture and history. Using religious terms, Heidegger maintains that Dasein is naturally in a state of "fallenness," a state in which "it" is absorbed in the forgetfulness and triviality of everyday life. In its fallenness, Dasein garners its identity and sense of being from "the crowd." I use quotation marks around the "it" because, as mentioned, Heidegger was trying to fashion a vocabulary that eschewed the subject-object dichotomy. Our "fallenness" is like falling into a recliner and binge watching a TV series. Popcorn in hand, we are not haunted with questions about the meaning of life, but are in a state of forgetfulness. Then something shakes the crossbeams of our existence. Kierkegaard calls it "the jolt." For Heidegger, it was an existential awareness of death, our "outermost possibility." This bracing awareness, coupled with the angst that it brings, grabs us by the wrist and pulls us out of the crowd. The anxiety engulfs us and we fall out of our fallenness, perhaps like someone in a waiting room, waiting to discover whether or not her child will survive an open-heart surgery. Strictly speaking, she is not alone but is surrounded by

This bracing awareness of death, coupled with the angst that it brings, grabs us by the wrist and pulls us out of the crowd.

people thumbing through magazines and saying rosaries, but feels isolated in her terror, alone and without recourse. Through a small window, she glimpses the surgeon walk by and thinks that even though he has just been touching her little girl's heart, the doctor is probably thinking of something like calling his wife to see how junior did at his basketball game. Again, anxiety—and death anxiety in particular—individuates us, makes us homesick for that recliner and forgetfulness. Yet, according to Kierkegaard, Heidegger, Tolstoy, and other existentialists, the anxiety, the homesickness, affords an opportunity for us to enter into an authentic relation with others and ourselves. In a gloss on Heidegger and Tolstoy, philosopher Mike Martin writes:

> Unconfronted, death is dreadful. It generates vague fears and anxieties that drive us away from authenticity and toward immersion in conventionality and everyday pleasures. . . . In fully acknowledging death we are pressured to unify our lives.[5]

And perhaps unifying our lives has something to do with being authentic.

While there is no unequivocal definition of *authenticity*, there is more to authenticity than refraining from putting on airs. I am acquainted with many individuals whom I would not describe as authentic even though they are devoid of pretenses solely on account of a cold indifference to the opinions of others. To become authentic is to become yourself. When Nietzsche implores, "Become who you are," like Heidegger he is prodding us to create ourselves. For Nietzsche, Sartre, and Heidegger, we are a witch's brew of culture, feelings, experiences, and evaluations, and we create ourselves out of this mélange, as though our lives were an artwork.

To become authentic is to become yourself.

Kierkegaard was emphatic that somewhere beneath our historically and culturally influenced vision of ourselves, there is a true self. As Dylan tells it, "You may be an ambassador to England or France . . . / But you're gonna have to serve somebody," and, for Kierkegaard, that servant is the real you. Authenticity is not to be confused with bucket lists or self-fulfillment. You might be a Picasso who realized every grain of your potential, but from a Kierkegaardian perspective, that doesn't mean you have become *authentic*, that you have become your true self, the self God meant you to be. But who is Kierkegaard to say? Why should I believe that the Creator of the universe created little old me with a plan that I must choose between trying to realize or ignoring? Maybe that plan is the same for us all: to love and look after our neighbor as we would ourselves, to be a good Samaritan. Am I to take this on a leap of faith? Take him or leave him, Kierkegaard held that a person's primary relationship is to God and from that, all other relationships properly follow.

For the spiritually squeamish, however, Kierkegaard opens another vista on authenticity. Traditionally, knowledge is defined as true justified belief. Kierkegaard was more about belief than he was about the issue of truth and justification. For Kierkegaard, the "how" was equally as important as the "what." Etymologically speaking, both in the Latin and German, the idea of authenticity is intrinsically bound up with the notion of making something your own. Kierkegaard believed that we make our views our own not by hitting "like" on Facebook but by passionately relating ourselves to those ideas and expressing them in the medium of action. Carry on about universal love and you had better be ready to make sacrifices to help the homeless woman sleeping on the grate in front of your apartment.

During the civil rights movement of the 1960s, there were many who spoke against the injustice of racism. The Freedom Riders not only spoke but acted. They rambled on buses down South to register voters. They knew the maelstrom of violence that they were driving into. Buses were bombed. They were often beaten within an inch of their lives and sometimes beyond that inch. All the while, the police in places like Jackson, Mississippi, either participated or stood arms akimbo, and let the frothing mob have at it with fists and clubs. Many of the protesters who boarded those southbound Greyhounds were first-generation college students. Their parents had to dig deeply to send them to college, but in order to participate in the freedom rides, these nineteen- and twenty-year-olds had to skip their exams and drop out or take a leave of absence from college. That was authenticity on two counts. They were not taking their marching orders from their parents or society in general, and they were acting on their convictions.

The view of the virtues embedded in existentialism often returns to the requirement to be honest with oneself. And authenticity requires that we be candid with ourselves as to whether or not we have truly appropriated the opinions that we might be slapped on the back for espousing.

Some days I whisper to myself, "Gordon, you always talk as though you are a devotee of kindness. Okay then, have you denied yourself anything for anyone today?" I want to be as kind to myself as I would be to a friend, but honestly there are times when I can't come up with a single thing that I have done to go out of my way for anyone. I am no Freedom Rider. Perhaps that indicates that I ought to consider the possibility that my convictions about kindness are a story I tell myself about myself that may not be as close to my heart as I would like to imagine. The view of the virtues embedded in existentialism often returns to the requirement to be honest with oneself. And authenticity requires that we be candid with ourselves as to whether or not we have truly appropriated the opinions that we might be slapped on the back for espousing.

And yet, to return to an earlier point, it could be argued that there were millions of Nazis who did just that, and hundreds of thousands of Americans who gave their last breath defending slavery. Is authenticity qua "being true to ourselves" a selfish and narcissistic ideal? Taylor writes:

> If authenticity is being true to ourselves, is recovering our own "*sentiment de l'existence*," then perhaps we can only achieve it integrally if we recognize that this sentiment connects us to a wider whole. It was perhaps not an accident that in the Romantic period the self-feeling and the feeling of belonging to nature were linked.[6]

Authenticity does not ensure moral rectitude, but Taylor suggests "perhaps the loss of a sense of belonging through a publicly defined order needs to be compensated by a stronger more inner sense of linkage." Kierkegaard would tab Taylor's stronger sense of "inner linkage" "inwardness," an ideal that Kierkegaard charged had been forgotten in his own age, and maybe all the more so in our age. With the emphasis on owning actions and choices, authenticity can seem selfishly self-referential. However, relational creatures that we are, it could be that becoming our own person is only possible vis-à-vis strong bonds to something outside of ourselves. For Kierkegaard it is God, but Taylor submits this connection can take the form of binding yourself to a "political cause or tending to the earth." In the early 1990s Taylor was more than hinting that we are living in an increasingly fragmented world. He submits, "Perhaps this is what a great deal of modern poetry has been trying to articulate."

Of his chosen disciple from Cana, Nathanael, Jesus said, "Here truly is an Israelite in whom there is no deceit" or guile. A person with nothing up his sleeves, a person who is just what he seems to be; perhaps, even, an "authentic" individual. However we define it, authenticity does not seem to be something we can work at, save in the sense that we can make strides to avoid inauthenticity. Rather than trying to seem like a fellow tough guy during my conversation with Mike Tyson, I could have tapped him on the shoulder and confessed that even though I answered the bell a few times, he and I did not inhabit similar worlds. Such an admission would have involved stripping myself of my armor and accepting a degree of vulnerability.

However we define it, authenticity does not seem to be something we can work at, save in the sense that we can make strides to avoid inauthenticity.

And yet, over and above refraining from "trying to seem," we have visited the notion that authenticity is a matter of becoming your true self. Even "The Poet" Shakespeare wrote, "To thine own self be true." The either-or, however, is this: Is that self a self we create or, à la Kierkegaard, a plan of a self that is there from the start, one that you can fail to realize even as you conquer territories, move mountains, or practice your own version of Minnesota Nice?

CHAPTER
5

FAITH

I don't exactly keep a gratitude journal, but when the black dog is ripping at my throat, I remind myself that my children, now grown men, are healthy, flourishing, and decent people. I take note that I am not living in poverty or a refugee camp or stepping over IEDs in Afghanistan. Now and again, as I am trying to reassure myself, there resounds a menacing internal voice saying, "If you are really looking for something to cry about, just wait." Sometimes, I torture myself with the thought that I ought to be able to savor the beauty of the present, but, when the gloom wafts in, beauty is just an abstraction.

One morning when the grief had its claws in me, I was

trudging along the railroad tracks by the river bend. Just a few feet away, perched on a low limb, was a bald eagle. In its majesty, it would have taken anyone else's breath away, but given the way I was feeling, it might as well have been a sparrow or a plastic bag caught up in the electrical wires. And that is how it was on a late spring afternoon a few months ago. I had just finished an informal counseling session at the college, giving a pep talk to one of my male students, trying to get him to toughen up and learn to battle through his depression, instead of skipping class day after day and then hating himself for his lack of self-control. I am not sure why, but afterward, I was feeling so out of joint, so alienated, that I needed something to douse the cold fire. It was the end of the day and I planned a pit stop at a local beer den on the way home.

Behind the wheel, headed to the altar with the neon Bud Lite sign in the window, something got into me and I found myself impulsively turning into St. Dominic's, the Catholic church in town. Raising my eyebrows as though I had been kidnapped, I reassured myself that I would soon be lifting the chalice of a brew, but there I was in church, in a near catatonic funk.

I was raised Catholic. Though my parents made sure I was confirmed and made it to church most Sundays, they were not especially devout. Maybe it was the influence of my beloved Italian nonna who lived with us, with all her statues and those rosaries perpetually in her hands, worn so soft from crocheting for eighty years, but as a third grader I would frequently get up before school and bike to morning mass. It had been decades, but there I was, back at church. It wasn't morning, and I wasn't a kid on a bike any longer, musing about my baseball card collection, but a gray beard with ghosts endlessly rounding the bases behind my eyes, a lost soul of less-than-little faith.

St. Dom's has a small chapel tucked away in a corner, an alcove where you can strike candles for the sick and deceased. Like a bar, it is a quiet, pleasantly dark, red-carpeted oasis with the addition of a tiny altar and a pale blue stained-glass-window depiction of the Virgin Mary. Pleased that no one else was there, I shambled up to the candleholder and slumped to my knees to light a candle for my long-deceased father. It seemed impossible, but all the glass cups were empty; all the candles had been burned down to the metal-clasped wick. After a second pass, I literally hissed a "WTF." The fact that I couldn't so much as light a candle for my old man sparked a paranoid sense that there was no benevolent higher power, but rather some fate-like dark force barreling across the universe, bent on grinding me into someone I would not care to glimpse in the mirror. Given my past transgressions, the punishment seemed to fit the crimes. I laughed at myself for stopping at the church and blamed this dastardly destiny for making me "lose my faith."

And yet, as I burst out of the heavy glass church doors,

a strange question swam up and broke the surface: Do we lose our faith or push it away?

It certainly felt as though some beastly hammer blows had knocked the spiritual breath—my hope and my prayers—out of me. But maybe not. Perhaps losing your faith is not like losing a set of keys. Maybe my inability to cope with the inevitable slings of suffering was responsible for not being able to cleave to the idea of the holy. But there I had been, at church on a late weekday afternoon, even though the idea that there is a personal God "up there" seemed utterly nonsensical. Bizarre squared seemed the notion that the Almighty sent his only Son, born of the Virgin Mary, and so on.

And yet, as I burst out of the heavy glass church doors, a strange question swam up and broke the surface: Do we lose our faith or push it away?

There have been times when I have tried to bolster my pearly gate prospects by reciting the idea that there are scientific claims demanding as much imagination to believe as the miracles of the Bible. Take black holes or parallel universes—or quarks, which exist in space and time but have no definite position. Strange, to say the least. No matter, as baffling as these phenomena might be, they still seemed less of a stretch than the Virgin Birth and the resurrection. After all, it is easy to understand why I might yearn for the Lazarus story to be true, but there is no such wish animating my quark convictions. Worse yet, the bizarre scientific claims are open to empirical testing and, if need be, revision; not so for the likes of the resurrection. Some philosophers have suggested that since there are no objective tests for determining whether or not God exists, we might settle the question on moral grounds. William James, the American giant and melancholic, found his will to believe along these pragmatic lines. James reasoned that if your life depended on needing to leap across a chasm, you would be much more likely to make a successful jump if you believed you could make the jump. Transformed to a grand scale, has religion had a positive moral impact on human history? What to compare it with? I am not sure; given the multitude of demonic deeds done in the name of variously named deities, I am hard-pressed to form a strong conviction that faith has been an elevating force; an ambiguous force, yes (after all, the civil rights movement came out of the churches), but not an altogether good one. By the same token, Hitler, Stalin, Mao, and Pol Pot were all atheists of the fundamentalist stripe. Ultimately, the moral criterion is not much help in resolving the ultimate either-or.

In a history of philosophy class last semester, we were mulling over Anselm's ontological argument. Philosophers classify Anselm's reasoning as a reductio ad absurdum argument. With this strategy, you assume the premises of the position that you are challenging and demonstrate that those premises lead to a contradiction. Logic dictates that a premise leading to a contradiction must be false. Anselm's ingenious argument begins, "the fool says in his heart that God does not exist" but even the fool agrees that if there were a God, it would be a being greater than which cannot be conceived. *Pace* Anselm, the idea of a being that exists in reality is greater than the idea of a being that exists only in the mind. Therefore, when the fool denies God's existence, he is not denying the existence of a being that only exists in the mind, for that would not be a being greater than which cannot be conceived. In sum, the atheist cannot deny God's existence without contradicting his conception of God. Ergo, God must exist.

After defying my befuddled students to find something amiss with the proof, I discussed a defect in Anselm's reasoning, then served up my rote-memorized Kierkegaardian line that if faith could be grounded in reason, there would be no need for faith. As my usual rift went, "Faith is a matter of believing in the unseen and unproven. You can't climb to heaven on a ladder of syllogisms, on the likes of the ontological argument." Most of them nodded, but a bright first year respectfully took me and Kierkegaard to task, pressing, "Doc, I don't understand. Why would the Creator provide us with reason and then put himself beyond reason? It doesn't make any sense."

Augustine, Aquinas, and a gaggle of other apologists have generated sophisticated answers to that simple and honest query, but I confess I have never found them compelling. It does appear preposterous that God would endow us with reason and at the same time lurk behind the curtain of intelligibility. Naturally, "the beyond reason" ploy is convenient for those who repose in the belief that they are under the aegis of a personal savior with superpowers. I had one such individual in my class, a student with a boundless yearning for God.

"Doc, I don't understand. Why would the Creator provide us with reason and then put himself beyond reason? It doesn't make any sense."

His name was Karan, a strict Hindu of nineteen. He was slight, dark, and had a red bindi for a third eye. His father was from India and managed a gas station in Chicago. A coruscating beacon of hope for his family, Karan's burning ambition was to become a religious teacher, a swami. Virtually every afternoon, Karan would come to my office and in a barely detectable Indian accent, badger me with questions about the relation between our philosophy texts and God or, in his case, as a Hindu, the gods. Karan was blessed with a restless and relentless longing for the divine. Tests gave him a serious case of nerves, so much so that even before an inconsequential quiz, he would pester me to go over questions he already had an iron-clad grip on. One time, I ribbed him, "Karan, you have to learn how to deal with anxiety. If you are going to be a swami, people are going to need you to help them when they are upset and afraid." Dropping his eyes, he answered with palpable earnestness, "You're right, Doc. I have to learn to deal with my anxiety."

The past tense that I have been using makes the tragic truth plain: Karan is of the past tense. A month before the end of the semester, he went to the clinic for a cold. He was given some antibiotics. When his condition failed to improve, the medical priests ran some tests. A month later, Hindu priests were bowing over his body with oils and flower petals, preparing Karan for cremation. Trusting in the gods, he did not cling to life even when he faced the non-negotiable fact that the future he had so passionately and meticulously mapped out was not to be. An angry part of me felt that if there happens to be a God, Karan was the last flower he should have plucked. Another part of me, however, felt that taking him made perfect sense since he was already more spirit than flesh and bone. After Karan's funeral, out in the parking lot of faith, I felt I could just as easily believe in Vishnu, Jesus, or the great god Nada.

If Camus happened to be there on the sad but sun-sparkling June afternoon of the funeral, I'm sure he would have counseled, "Go ahead, roll around in the dirt with your grief and rage, but unless you are enjoying yourself doing it, give up puzzling about the meaning of Karan's death and everything else." In his unique combination of objectivity and lyricism, Camus contends that we are creatures with an innate, esurient desire for meaning pitched into a universe devoid of meaning. For Camus, the conflict between our need for meaning and a meaningless world is the absurd. Shakespeare's Macbeth was no idiot when he shook his fist and howled that life "is a tale told by an idiot, full of sound and fury, signifying nothing." Camus's existential prescription is that we accept the futility of our innermost desires and remain faithful to that recognition of the absurd.

The genius of the literary wing of the existential tradition is that those authors seldom leave us with an abstraction without an attending concrete example drawn from life or fiction. In *The Myth of Sisyphus*, Camus serves up a fresh rendition of an ancient tale. The King of Ephyra, Sisyphus, dies and is in the underworld. Sly and endearing, he wrangles the gods into allowing him to return to the earth

---

Camus contends that we are creatures with an innate, esurient desire for meaning pitched into a universe devoid of meaning. Camus's existential prescription is that we accept the futility of our innermost desires and remain faithful to that recognition of the absurd.

---

in order to punish his wife for dishonoring him. The gods concede, but having exacted his revenge, Sisyphus cannot bring himself to leave "the curve of the gulf, the sparkling sea, and smiles of earth." Having lost patience, the gods send Mercury out to recapture Sisyphus and return him to the kingdom of the dead. Once returned, the gods punish Sisyphus by compelling him for all time to roll a rock up a mountain, only to watch that same rock tumble back down again. The former fugitive from the underworld is carrying out his sentence to this day and probably in a dim light, but does Camus's Sisyphus complain? "The lucidity that was to constitute his torture," Camus writes, "at the same time crowns his victory. There is no fate that cannot be surmounted by scorn. . . . I leave Sisyphus at the foot of the mountain! One always finds one's burden again. But Sisyphus teaches the higher fidelity that negates the gods and raises rocks. He too concludes that all is well."[1]

Consciousness of the absurd is supposed to remove the sting from the absurd. The gospel according to Camus teaches that denizens of death row, which means all of us, should be freed from the fetters of worries about figuring out the *best* kind of life. The cosmos is chaos. There is no right way to live: "one life is as good as another" and just as meaningless.

Camus's muse, Nietzsche, warned that when you look into the abyss too long the abyss looks back and through you. Arthur Schopenhauer, Nietzsche's muse, grumbled:

> In early youth, we sit before the impending course of our life like children at the theater before the curtain is raised, who sit there in happy and excited expectation of the things that are to come. It is a blessing that we do not know what will actually come. For to the man who knows, the children may at times appear to be like the innocent delinquents who are condemned not to death, it is true, but to life and have not yet grasped the purport of their sentence.[2]

Acknowledging the absurdity of existence is unnerving enough for some to put their head in a noose and for others to commit what Camus termed "philosophical suicide." Those who figuratively strangle themselves escape the feeling of absurdity by imagining there is something transcendent, something in Plato's heaven or in the Judeo-Christian hereafter that will make sense of the toil and moil of the fact that we battle for years, struggle to make our daily bread, are lanced with loss, grief, heartbreak, then suddenly, all is over, we are gone. For what? I recently visited a friend's grave; for a moment the little city of the dead loomed up like a plain of collapsed universes, a nicely cropped field of black holes of subjectivity with buoy-like gravestones floating above them.

Hordes of happy wanderers whistle as they skip down that short or long hall in and out of existence. Viktor Frankl, a survivor of Auschwitz and founder of logotherapy, lived by Nietzsche's adage, "If you can find a why, you can find a how." The deuce with Camus. There are throngs who can talk themselves into the idea that they have a purpose on this planet, and just as many others who are not bedeviled by the need for a purpose, who can find purpose enough in playing with their children, potluck dinners, pruning their tomato plants, and the like. Among those too distracted to go under the hypnotic spell of daily life, there is no one, according to Camus, who could discern more deeply the empty core of existence than Kierkegaard. Thus, Camus shakes his head with disapproval, as if to complain that the writer who taught that it is only by the power of the absurd that we can have faith was by virtue of that faith unable to maintain a faithful awareness of the absurd. Camus concludes that Kierkegaard and a phalanx of other seers have committed intellectual hari-kari by first recognizing human existence for the madhouse that it is, and then mentally constructing an apparatus like faith in God to put everything in order and make some semblance of sense of their lives.

There is a page that resonates with Camus's reading of Kierkegaard. In *Fear and Trembling*, Kierkegaard's pseudonym Johannes de Silentio writes:

> If a human being did not have an eternal consciousness, if underlying everything there were only a wild, fermenting power that writhing in dark passions produced everything, be it significant or insignificant, if

a vast, never appeased emptiness hid beneath everything, what would life be then but despair? If such
were the situation, if there were no sacred bond that
knit humankind together, if one generation emerged
after another like forest foliage, if one generation succeeded another like the singing of birds in the forest,
if a generation passed through the world as a ship
through the sea, as wind through the desert, an un-
thinking and unproductive performance, if an eternal
oblivion, perpetually hungry, lurked for its prey and
there were no power strong enough to wrench that
away from it—how empty and devoid of consolation
life would be![3]

And then comes the string of words that, for Camus,
amount to philosophical suicide. Kierkegaard adds, "But
precisely for that reason it is not so"; that is, there is a God
who watches over us and therefore life is good.

It is a secular one, but I have a confession to make. One
of my go-to narratives has long been that Kierkegaard came
to my rescue at a time when I didn't much care whether I
lived or disappeared. Though dead for 150-plus years, Kierkegaard was a therapist of mine. Much of his therapy took
the form of spurring me in the direction of taking faith
more seriously. Forgive me, "Taking faith more seriously"
rings as though I were referring to a thesis; that way of expressing it is dead wrong. Kierkegaard resurrected whatever

vague longing it was that had me pedaling my bike to early morning mass fifty-five years ago. I am all too human, and once the minor miracle took place and my seas calmed, I tended to forget about the peace that I had prayed for and, to some extent, been granted.

Though dead for 150-plus years, Kierkegaard was a therapist of mine. Much of his therapy took the form of spurring me in the direction of taking faith more seriously.

Dostoyevsky defined human beings as "ungrateful bipeds." Kierkegaard concurs. In *The Sickness unto Death*, Kierkegaard sketches a situation in which our worst nightmare materializes. We pray and are saved by what we think could only be a miracle, and then a few days or weeks later, we go back over the event and shrug, "Ah, it must have been a coincidence."

For another example of the iron law of ingratitude: One night in the early 1970s, I had a sinuous six-footer rush down a block in Manhattan and, for reasons I will never understand, try to bash my brains in with a hefty Louisville Slugger. I was no brick-breaking black belt, but as the bat was about to crash into my skull, I snapped my forearm up and the bat splintered in half. Agog, my assailant sprinted off sure that Superman was on his trail. Shocked that I was still vertical, I was gratefully thinking, "Someone up there must have been watching over me." The days passed, and rewinding the scene I slowly began to suspect that the miracle of the parting of the bat was just a lucky, freak accident.

Most of Kierkegaard's Danish compadres thought of him as a brilliant but overwrought religious fanatic. Kierkegaard's most outright rigorously religious works were published in the late 1840s and early 1850s—volumes such as *Practice in Christianity* and his *Attack on Christendom*. Even today, Danes tend to pooh-pooh these volumes as though they were the feverish product of a religious pathology. They are not alone, many if not most of the scholars who commit their intellectual lives to poring over Kierkegaard's works use all their acumen trying to pry Kierkegaard's psychological epiphanies away from their pietistic moorings. Even in this book, I am not entirely innocent of maneuvers intended to counter resistance to the religious. In a way, it is an odd testimony to Kierkegaard's genius that he could speak to so many moderns/postmoderns who otherwise find talk of Christ silly and boorish. It would be as if evangelicals were to gain inspiration from Nietzsche or Marx.

To be sure, Kierkegaard is uplifting in his own right. He is able to catch us out in all our variegated acts of moral evasion. And yet the rat hole that he is most urgently concerned with plugging is that of neglecting our God relationship. If the depth psychologists are correct, and Kierkegaard was certainly one of them, then on many matters we can't honestly say, "I believe this or that." We are multilayered creatures who might think one thing at one level and something different at another, unconscious level. For all my sneering at the idea of the empty tomb, every time I have been shuddering in one of life's foxholes, be it a near-fatal car crash, heart surgery, or cancer in the family, the doubts were muted and the paternosters were on my lips. Freudians would chuckle: "Of course they were. We all crave protection and reassurance." Then again, it would be a genetic fallacy to conclude that because I want something to be true it must be false; just because my belief in God stems from a need for God, it doesn't follow that God does not exist. On the other hand, my desire for protection is hardly positive evidence of an almighty protector. Back and forth I go like a doubly doubting Thomas, but where faith is concerned, the going forth has always been with Kierkegaard's palm on my shoulder.

Were it not for Kierkegaard who, as a boy, was nicknamed "The Fork" for his ability to find a person's weak spots and stick it to them, I doubt I would have stopped at church that afternoon. I doubt I would be whispering a prayer whenever the spirit and neurons move me. Every line of fracture in the vast edifice of Kierkegaard's thought traces straight or zigzags back to God. When well performed, mockery is more effective than counterargument. Sometimes, it was just Kierkegaard's sidelong glances, revealing the smug, spiritlessness of modern ways of thinking and being that lit a match under my shoe. Take this one, aimed at those who never give a thought to developing the continuity Kierkegaard associates with becoming your true self:

> There is a story about a peasant who went barefooted to town with enough money to buy himself a pair of stockings and shoes and to get drunk, and in trying to find his way home in a drunken state, he fell asleep in the middle of the road. A carriage came along, and the driver shouted to him to move or he would drive over his legs. The drunken peasant woke up, looked over his legs and, not recognizing them because of the shoes and stockings, said: "Go ahead, they are not my legs."[4]

Kierkegaard's supernal satirical abilities would not have been enough to prompt me to read the Bible for the first time in eons as something other than an "interesting" literature. More important than his daedal use of irony was his compelling understanding of what it means to try to be faithful.

In *Fear and Trembling*, Kierkegaard offers a reading of Genesis 22, the story of Abraham and the binding of Isaac. Published in 1843, this work is aimed at retrieving what the then thirty-year-old Kierkegaard sometimes referred to as the "primitivity" of faith. Abraham is universally praised as the "father of faith" and yet he was poised to commit the most heinous crime. Through this tale of the binding of Isaac (known as the *Akedah* in the Jewish tradition), Kierkegaard attempts to prick awareness of the fact that faith is not all about cozy holiday gatherings; faith is something that both attracts and repels. Hearing a voice, Abraham believed that God had commanded him to take his son Isaac to Mount Moriah and offer him as a sacrifice. If God's edict did not create a "teleological suspension of the ethical," that is, if God's command did not allow for the suspension of morals, then, claims Kierkegaard, we should stop praising Abraham and call him what he is: "a murderer." *Fear and Trembling* indirectly reveals that religion cannot be reduced to the ethical, since there was no ethical justification for what Abraham was poised to do. Raising the knife to slit his little boy's throat was not something the "father of faith" intended for the greater good of the community. It was a private affair, or, as Kierkegaard states it, "Abraham did it for God's sake and his own sake." Abraham put himself, the individual, above the universal, above the community. He was willing to sacrifice Isaac, but the marvel is that because of God's promise that Abraham's offspring would be the head of many nations, Abraham fully expected to receive Isaac back; though, how so is far from clear.

Scrutinizing the same text, Kant commented that Abraham should have reasoned that it was more likely that Abraham was hearing voices and had gone off the deep end than that an all-good and all-powerful God would order him to murder his son! Though he deeply respected Kant, the Kierkegaard of *Fear and Trembling* did not portray the father of faith as someone whose life was guided by probability calculations. Like Job, Abraham was being tested by God, and like Job he aced the exam. Sensible people sensibly wonder what kind of sadistic deity would command a person to kill his son and then, as if he were only joking, retract the command.

Abraham's *movement of faith* is "paradoxical" in that it is one of simultaneously giving up the world (Isaac) and expecting it back. This spiritual triple axel is a pure contradiction. Kierkegaard frequently brings to mind how big the little word "if" is, but *if* faith has any legitimacy and if we can use a spatial metaphor, faith is something beyond or to the side of reason. Since the movement of faith and, ultimately, its object are paradoxical, faith cannot be comprehended, which is tantamount to saying, that *if* faith has any validity, it cannot be unpacked in terms of reason; it cannot be understood as a set of stories for edification or as a kind of philosophy for dummies.

Many who have dismissively waved off the "God stuff" have been unable to tuck away their longing for "something deeper." Some of these religiously skeptical seekers now look to philosophers as a priest class uniquely capable of opening the trapdoor to that deeper something. The shibboleth of the philosophers is "What is your argument?"

Sorry to disappoint, but there is no argument from Kierkegaard for faith. In fact, he warns that offering a defense of faith is a sin against faith, akin to offering a brief to prove that you love your spouse. Like an open window on a brisk autumn day, Kierkegaard's honesty is singularly refreshing. In more ways than ten, Kierkegaard acknowledges that faith involves a collision with the understanding. He was clear that neither the ontological nor any other form of argument will turn the water of unbelief into the wine of faith. It is a truism, but for most of history humans invoked divinities to cope with enigmas now explained by science. As science advanced, the need for God ebbed, as though God were some type of theory. Kierkegaard thrived in an era of scientific efflorescence, and yet for him faith was not an explanation. He offers no objective reasons for turning your existence over to an invisible God. When St. Paul preached about Jesus and everlasting life to the Stoics, those paragons of reason laughed and suspected that Paul was drunk. From a Kierkegaardian point of view, they had a right to laugh. Christian faith is an offense to the understanding.

In more ways than ten, Kierkegaard acknowledges that faith involves a collision with understanding. He was clear that neither the ontological nor any other form of argument will turn the water of unbelief into the wine of faith.

Theologically speaking, one of Kierkegaard's signal contributions was tethering the possibility of faith to the possibility of offense. Remember, Jesus begged those he encountered, "Do not be offended by me." After all, there he was, a homeless man from the laboring class telling priests and others that he was the Son of God and—much more radical yet—that he could forgive sins. In his very flesh, Jesus was an insult to reason. For Kierkegaard, approaches to Jesus that abnegate this offense (à la Jesus was a sage with a message about teaching us to love one another) annul the need for and possibility of faith. Without offense, there would be no need for faith; there would be no need for anything other than knowledge. No pantheist, it is as if Kierkegaard construed offense as God's way of keeping us at an arms distance, of telling us that while God is with us, there is also a chasmal difference between us, the difference between innocence and sin.

Today, we worship autonomy. Years ago, obedience was a quality that was always included among the virtues. No longer. If we find anything offensive today, it is the notion of being told what to do or who to be. In his *The Sickness unto Death*, Kierkegaard, the high priest of existentialism and choice, asserted that where there is no authority there is no obedience, and where there is no obedience there is no seriousness. Kierkegaard's positive framing of authority and obedience provide such an untimely message that very few Kierkegaard devotees take note of it.

Theologically speaking, one of Kierkegaard's signal contributions was tethering the possibility of faith to the possibility of offense. Without offense, there would be no need for faith; there would be no need for anything other than knowledge.

Readers who have hit the religion off switch will surely find Kierkegaard's ruminations a kind of malarkey, but there is worse to come. The charge of narcissism is tossed around too freely these days; nevertheless, we live in an age that puts such inordinate emphasis on feeling good about yourself that one often has to be wary of offering even gently constructive criticism. And then comes Kierkegaard and his insistence that much more than needing a revelation to know that we are saved, we need an experience on the road to Damascus to know that we are sinners. We need a revelation to understand what it *means* that we are sinners. This is not exactly the power of positive thinking, but according to Kierkegaard, we need God to teach us how thoroughly depraved we are. Faith is the opposite of sin, and paradoxically it requires faith to understand we are sinners.

Know thyself? Not on our own. Maybe he was overwrought, but Kierkegaard no less than Dostoyevsky believed that self-transparency is impossible without faith. In addition to self-honesty, the self-knowledge that Socrates trumpeted demands thinking about your life in the correct categories. As I have argued, when we roll back our eyes and look inward, the way we tease apart our inner lives is largely determined by the concepts we use to identify those happenings in the private theater of our skull. If my ultimate categories of analysis are psychodynamic, I might interpret my nasty inner dialogues as the internalized voice of angry authority figures. From a neuroscientific point of view, I might read the same self-scarification process as an indication that my serotonin tank is low. From a Marxist perspective, my inner-directed rage might be understood as a reaction to exploitation and class differences. Seen through the prism of Kierkegaardian religious categories, a beastly attitude toward myself is probably best interpreted as a prideful refusal to let God in and accept forgiveness.

Again, there are different levels of self-understanding. I could understand the funk that I was in when I stopped to

---

Maybe he was overwrought, but Kierkegaard no less than Dostoyevsky believed that self-transparency is impossible without faith. In addition to self-honesty, the self-knowledge that Socrates trumpeted demands thinking about your life in the correct categories.

try to light a candle for my father as a function of both past experiences and neurochemistry. Who is to say what the right terms of self-understanding are? Who is to say what the ultimate categories for self-examination are? I can't imagine what a decisive answer to that question might look like. It all depends on your presuppositions about the self.

Philosophers from Hume onward regard the very idea of the self as bordering on a fiction. In sharp contrast, Kierkegaard is a true believer in the self as an entity and as a task. It is, Kierkegaard claimed, no surprise that there is no universal definition of the self because the self is a particular, and "no science can say what the self is without again stating it quite generally. And this is the wonder of life, that each man who is mindful of himself knows what no science knows, since he knows who he himself is."[5] It is our sacred and appointed duty "to become our true self," which the Kierkegaard of *The Sickness unto Death* equates with becoming a *true human being*, a spirit. Again, the little word *if*, but *if* Kierkegaard is correct, we can't wait for a nice, tidy definition of the self before taking up the task of trying to become ourselves. Take heed, says he, "The first thing to keep in mind is that every human being is an individual human being and is to become conscious of being an individual human being."[6] Here, however, is the Kierkegaardian rub: when you leave your relationship to God out of the picture, you can't help but leave your true self out of the picture as well.

Once again, with regard to faith and everything else Kierkegaardian, the accent is on passion and action. In a famous passage from his *Concluding Unscientific Postscript*, Kierkegaard asks the rhetorical question:

> If someone who lives in the midst of Christianity enters, with knowledge of the true idea of God, the house of God, the house of the true God, and prays, but prays in untruth, and if someone lives in an idolatrous land but prays with all the passion of infinity, although his eyes are resting upon the image of an idol—where, then, is there more truth? The one prays in truth to God although he is worshipping an idol; the other prays in untruth to the true God and is therefore in truth worshipping an idol.[7]

With regard to faith and everything else Kierkegaardian, the accent is on passion and action.

The pagan has more faith than the man who drags himself to church for appearance's sake and goes back and forth between thoughtlessly mumbling prayers and trying to interpret the meaning of an ambiguous remark that his boss let fly on Friday. The pagan also has more faith than the fanatic who relates to his religious convictions as though they were scientific truths. As for that rigidly orthodox individual:

> He talks of meeting before the throne of God and knows how many times one should bow. He knows everything, like the man who can prove a mathematical proposition when the letters are ABC, but not when the letters are DEF.[8]

In *Postscript*, Kierkegaard proclaims, "where there is certainty, there is no faith." Or again, where there is certainty, there is no risk, and "where there is no risk, there is no faith."

Though not so much with talking about Kierkegaard, there are enormous risks in taking Kierkegaard seriously in the personal, existential sense. To listen to Kierkegaard, becoming a follower of Christ means, well, trying to follow Christ. It means striving to imitate the life of Christ and so letting your attachments to the pleasure and laurels of this world die on the vine. Kierkegaard was up-front, even confessional, about the fact that it is one thing to poetize the movements of faith and quite another to make those movements. The Christian life that Kierkegaard beckons us to palls over some of the pleasures and thrills that we identify with feeling alive. Trying to address sex and sensuality from a spiritual point of view, Kierkegaard admits that when it comes to eros:

The spirit is indeed present . . . but it cannot express itself in the erotic. It feels itself a stranger. It says, as it were, to the erotic: My dear, in this I cannot be a third party; therefore I shall hide myself for the time being.[9]

Again, Christianity offers a cold hand to many of the joys and pleasures that seem to make life worth living. Indeed, one of the criticisms that Nietzsche leveled against Christianity was that it cultivated a suspicion about any- and everything connected with abundant pleasure.

In his famous "wager argument," Blaise Pascal (1623–1662) reasoned that since belief in God tenders an infinite gain against a finite loss, faith is a betting man's wager. Pascal did not imagine that belief itself would issue forth from the wager argument, but he hoped that it would at least convince people to go through the motions, taking the holy water and saying prayers. A behaviorist of sorts, Pascal believed that faith might follow along mechanically. While he held Pascal in high esteem, and is even sometimes described as "the Pascal of the North," Kierkegaard was not taken in by Pascal's reasoning.

Kierkegaard never used the exact phrase with which he has become nearly synonymous, that is, "the leap of faith." Nevertheless, faith for him was a dreadfully dangerous leap in which you just might be carelessly ditching the only life you have. In the arc of the leap is the trust that we possess an eternal element. Today, many Christians explain that you

do not need to believe or even have to try to believe in a
life after death to count yourself among the flock. These
same folks, many of them members of the clergy, will quote
St. Paul, and yet it was St. Paul who proclaimed, "If in this
life only we have hope in Christ, we are of all men most
miserable."

In Miguel de Unamuno's previously mentioned novella
Saint Manuel Bueno, Martyr, the protagonist and priest
Don Manuel lives a Christ-like existence, tirelessly tending to his mountain village flock. Though he conceals his
doubts from the villagers, Don Manuel cannot bring himself
to believe that there is any hope beyond this life. Because of
his certainty about the finality of death, Don Manuel sees
himself as an imposter and an apostate. Was he right?

Belief in the hereafter offends reason. It takes a powerful
imagination to cleave to the idea expressed in *The Sickness
unto Death* that "Christianly understood . . . death is by no
means the last of all; in fact, it is only a minor event within
that which is all, an eternal life." Christianly understood,
mindfulness classes won't do it; your inner peace is one
thing, believing that you have an eternal element is another
something that whispers you need "to die to this world"
to come alive. No wonder the Stoics enjoyed a good belly
laugh at Paul. Maybe it is too much, too improbable, and too
risky, and yet Kierkegaard wags a finger that there is grave
spiritual risk to being risk averse.

To return to the question that greeted me outside the church door—is faith something we passively lose, or is it something we tell ourselves we lose but un- or half-consciously push away? To be sure, there are millions who shruggingly dismiss faith as nonsense; millions who proudly proclaim that they have no need of God now or when they end up in the ICU. As the late Kierkegaard scholar David Kangas explained, the need for God for Kierkegaard is unlike other needs in that it does not reveal a lack. The need for God is a human being's highest perfection. It is a gift of the condition necessary for receiving the gift of faith in God. This sophisticated bit of ex-egesis is not likely to change the mind of someone convinced that it is tragic that so many otherwise rational beings could be taken in by such a patently false illusion as God.

For the holy fools who hanker for faith, feelings and con-victions wax and wane. A few days ago, I had to spend hours with a petulant individual who set my jaw on edge and made my skin crawl. I literally prayed for a soul softening. To my surprise, the afternoon spent together was almost pleasant. Driving home, I was musing that it felt as though someone had reached in and changed my heart. For a couple of hours, quirks that might have transformed me into the figure in Munch's famous painting *The Scream* were suddenly, mi-raculously, easy to gloss over and let pass. I also speculated about how difficult it is to detect miracles that only occurred inwardly. We always picture the miraculous as walking on water or healing the blind; how about as opening the sluices of loving feelings?

The decisive question about faith is how we relate to our beliefs and feelings. When you lack all conviction, do you chase after it or throw up your hands and say, "Thank God I have outgrown those superstitions"? But for not-so-holy fools like the present author, it seems perfectly fitting to pray to a God you don't believe in for faith in God. Dostoyevsky taught that the worry about faith is faith, and Kierkegaard, who likened prayer to listening to God, remarked, "Prayer does not change God, but it changes him who prays."

I suppose I should be chary of pinning this conviction on Kierkegaard, but in the decades I have spent hacking through the teeming jungle of his thoughts, I have come to think of faith as trust, the kind you might have in a friend or loved one. Where knowledge and a lack of certainty are the rule, trust would seem the most appropriate term. When existence slams the door on our fingers, we either wince and try to sustain trust in God, or we let go of him, as though God were a friend who betrayed us. But if we lose our faith, it is on purpose; it is our own doing.

But for not-so-holy fools like the present author, it seems perfectly fitting to pray to a God you don't believe in for faith in God. I have come to think of faith as trust, the kind you might have in a friend or loved one.

CHAPTER
6

MORALITY

Tests of moral mettle usually pounce on us without warning. A few days ago, a friend emailed saying that in the morning when he pulled up to drop his daughter off at her grammar school, he turned to see a man in the car next to him slapping his little boy around. Should my friend have intervened? There is no practice run. There you are and you have to decide on a moment's notice what to do, knowing in your bones that this isn't any ordinary choice, but a choice of what kind of person you will be, a choice of who you are.

I once went for what I suspected was going to be a sad but ordinary sickbed visit with a relative who had been a mentor to me for many years. Maybe I had been out of touch, but I soon grasped that for him, it was late in the fifth act. There were no longer any sources of pleasure in his life. He had severe heart problems and collapsed discs, which caused him relentless, agonizing back spasms. With nothing to placate the pain, his glaucous eyes were suffused with tears. A platoon of yellow pill bottles sat on a nearby shelf. One was filled with powerful opioids. It was twilight and his soft groans filled the room as he thought ahead to the long, lonely, excruciating night stretching before him. He sighed deeply and fell silent for a moment and then asked, "Gordon, pass me that bottle. I can't take it anymore."

What to do? I loved the man and knew there was only more misery ahead. Worse yet, when it comes to interminable suffering, I can't help but imagine that unyielding pain cauterizes good memories, chases them out of the house along with our most tender feelings. Without any hope of a respite, prolonged agony can numb a person, making him indifferent to what is closest to his heart. To me, it seems a death within a death. So what about the pills? His nurse would not be returning for another four hours. There would be plenty of time to help him through the door and out of the cage of his suffering. What to do?

Kierkegaard, using the pseudonym Johannes Climacus, wrote that unlike most scribblers, he took up his quill not to make life easier for his readers but to make it more difficult. Maybe that is how it is with morality. The more developed you become, the more moral issues you discern, the more taxing life becomes.

The existentialists are so riveted to the idea of unifying thought and action that it would be reasonable to expect that they would have developed some kind of ethical guide to help us distinguish between right and wrong. Not exactly. None of the authors with whom we are in conversation ever composed anything approximating a full-fledged moral theory. At the end of his *Being and Nothingness*, Jean-Paul Sartre promised a sequel in the form of an existential ethics. Though he lived nearly forty years after the publication of this tome, he failed to deliver his ethics book. Simone de Beauvoir, Sartre's lifetime lover, tried to make good on Sartre's promise with her *Ethics of Ambiguity*. While original in its own right, de Beauvoir's ethics was less than satisfying, even by her own reckoning. A friend of both Sartre's and de Beauvoir's, Camus confided that his instruction on matters moral did not come in the form of treatises but from his vocation as a football goal keeper. In an interview, Camus said, "After many years during which I saw many things, what I know most surely about morality and the duty of man I owe to sport . . ." Later he would add that his lessons in justice not only came from the soccer pitch but the theater as well.

Still, the paucity of ethical treatises or existential moral vade mecums does not imply that the existentialists are void of moral insights. I repeat, the love that philosophy refers to is not a love of knowledge but a love of wisdom, an understanding of how to live a moral and good life. Even Aristotle underscored that his *Nicomachean Ethics* was not about learning what virtue is but about becoming virtuous, becoming good. On that score, though the existentialists comprising the dramatis personae of this book may not have worked out systematic ethical theories, their writings bristle with moral epiphanies, a few of which I hope to share from Sartre, Nietzsche, Kierkegaard, and Camus.

I repeat, the love that philosophy refers to is not a love of knowledge but a love of wisdom, an understanding of how to live a moral and good life.

Midway in his "Existentialism Is a Humanism" essay, Sartre recalls the story of a young man who came to him for advice. The "boy," as Sartre refers to him, confides that his brother has been killed by the Nazis, and to avenge his death he wants to join the resistance. There is, however, a problem. Because the young man is the sole survivor in his family and his mother needs him, he has to choose between the resistance and his responsibilities at home. Aristotle taught that life is too rich and varied in circumstances to try to live according to a moral rule book. Sartre agrees:

Who could help him choose? Christian doctrine? No. Christian doctrine says, "Be charitable, love your neighbor, take the more rugged path, etc. . . . Whom should he love as a brother? The fighting man or his mother? Which does the greatest good, the vague act of fighting in a group, or the concrete one of helping a particular human being go on living? Who can decide *a priori*? Nobody. No book of ethics can tell him. The Kantian ethics says, "Never treat any person as a means, but as an end." Very well, if I stay with my mother, I'll treat her as an end and not as a means; but by virtue of this very fact, I am running the risk of treating the people around me who are fighting, as means.[1]

People frequently react to being in the vice of bad options, huffing, "I'll just go with my gut feelings." Sartre blocks this ploy, pointing out that we can talk deep into the night about our feelings and how much we hate hatred or love justice, but ultimately our conversations and the emotions infusing them are empty *without* action. Or, as Sartre puts it, "The only way to determine the value of this affection is, precisely, to perform an act which confirms and defines it." Forgive the platitude, but for Sartre, if you don't walk your talk, then it is just talk. Another common strategy is to seek out counsel when poised between right and wrong. Sartre dispatches that tactic as well, observing that

when we look about for advice, we inevitably turn to someone we think will tell us what we want to hear.

___

Forgive the platitude, but for Sartre, if you don't walk
your talk, then it is just talk.

___

Without any objective set of rules to guide our actions,
we still must choose. Neither a nihilist nor a moral relativ-
ist, Sartre emphatically states that we are responsible for our
actions. For him, being a human being in the deepest sense
demands the ability to abide with anxiety and despair—
anxiety because you are free, responsible, and devoid of
moral guideposts; and despair because there are no guaran-
tees about the outcomes of your struggles. Open your history books; over time, millions have fought for justice, and
both their causes and their bodies have been covered over
in mass graves. Sartre is not convinced of that long arc of
justice that Dr. King put his faith in and spoke about with
such power and fervor.

Both Kierkegaard and Sartre connected freedom, anxiety, and responsibility. With freedom comes the anxiety
needed to make morally responsible choices. Both thinkers
recognize a natural impulse to want to escape this burden-
some freedom. One of Sartre's most influential concepts,
which has worked itself into common parlance, is his notion

of "bad faith." To be in bad faith is to deny our freedom by acting as though we were objects. There are many patterns of bad faith, but at base Sartre insists that bad faith is a futile attempt to lie to oneself. In *Being and Nothingness*, he explains, "the one who practices bad faith is hiding a displeasing truth or presenting as truth a pleasing untruth." What makes bad faith different from an ordinary lie is "the fact that in bad faith it is from myself that I am hiding the truth." A few lines later, Sartre brings down the gavel: "Bad faith does not come from the outside to human reality. One does not undergo his bad faith, one is not infected with it, it is not a *state*. But consciousness infects itself with it."[2] Sartre, who was well-versed in Freud, took aim at psychoanalysis, charging that the psychoanalytic mind-set is an open invitation to bad faith in that it tempts us to imagine that we are not acting freely but at the behest of unconscious forces. I might, for instance, tell myself that I did not choose to respond to my brother with withering sarcasm; my vitriol was the expression of unconscious rage at my father. Or perhaps I tell myself that the reason I acted coolly with a friend struggling through a divorce was because my serotonin levels were out of whack. Sartre insists that we know we are lying to ourselves when we deny our ability to choose freely.

Recently, I watched a documentary about the tragic 1966 massacre at the University of Texas at Austin. On a searing August day, former Marine sharpshooter Charles Whitman climbed to the observation deck of the University of Texas tower and, over a period of ninety-six minutes, shot forty-eight passersby, mortally wounding seventeen. Early in his murderous spree, Whitman wounded a pregnant woman and killed her husband. There, before scores of people, the pregnant woman lay in 100-degree heat on the grill-like concrete. Watching her writhing in agony and distress, many bystanders were torn between their fear and the feeling that they had to pull the woman to safety. Half a century later, one woman recalled, "I wanted to help, but I knew then that I was a coward."

Sartre insists that we know we are lying to ourselves when we deny our ability to choose freely.

I knew that I was a coward? Not for Sartre. He writes, "But when the existentialist writes about a coward, he says that this coward is responsible for his cowardice. He is not like that because he has a cowardly heart or lung or brain; . . . he is like that because he has made himself a coward by his acts."[3] To convince yourself that you are a coward, according to Sartre, is to practice the bad faith of pretending that being a coward is akin to being born with blue eyes or blond hair. It is to convince yourself that you couldn't have acted other than in a cravenly fashion.

No one is born a coward or, for that matter, a hero. We only selectively want to believe it, but we can change. Moral U-turns are possible. It may not be the kind of narrative to have touched Sartre, but my favorite story in the New Testament is when Peter denies Jesus three times. After his final "I don't know him," you would have thought that Peter might have taken the Judas option. Instead, he recouped his courage, was crucified for his Lord, and became the rock of the church.

No one is born a coward or, for that matter, a hero. We only selectively want to believe it, but we can change. Moral U-turns are possible.

Though he regularly identified himself an immoralist, to say nothing of the Antichrist, Nietzsche was a passionate moralizer. He is most well-known and/or reviled for his announcement of the death of God, which is in effect a declaration of the impossibility of faith in the present age. However, for Nietzsche it isn't just God who died; our present morals are ghosts of values past. In his most lucid and accessible work, *On the Genealogy of Morals*, Nietzsche, like Marx and Freud but with different analysis and terminology, proclaims that the conscience, which we have been taught to believe is sacred, derives neither from God nor reason. Because conscience does not come from on high, Nietzsche maintained that it is imperative that we take a historical perspective on our moral principles. At the same time, he warns about the difficulties of adopting the historical "long view," in part because we are a product and part of the very process we aim to examine.

Cultivating a historical perspective on ethics requires undertaking a "genealogy of morals." We need to decipher how our moral concepts have evolved, or perhaps devolved, over the millennia. A philologist, that is, someone who studies the origins of words, Nietzsche tracks the vicissitudes of meaning of normative concepts such as good and evil, while simultaneously underscoring the fact that over time, new meanings, often antithetical to the original, emerge. Still, the old connotations live on as feint resonances. For example, students today blithely use *sucks* as a pejorative. They are incredulous when I inform them of the sexual connotations of this now commonly used word in the not-too-remote 1970s.

More pertinent to Nietzsche's point, we currently associate goodness with peace, kindness, and justice. This was not always so. Not by a long shot. Nietzsche submits:

> I believe I may venture to interpret the Latin *bonus* [good] as "the warrior" provided I am right in tracing *bonus* back to an earlier *duonus*. . . . Therefore *bonus* as the man of strife, of dissention (*duo*), as the man

of war: one sees what constituted the "goodness" of a man in ancient Rome. Our German *gut* [good] even: does it not signify "the godlike," the man of "godlike race"? And is it not identical with the popular (originally noble) name of the Goths?"[4]

The radical shift into the present pacific nexus of meanings was the result of what Nietzsche terms the "slave revolt." As this tale goes, back in the days of who knows exactly when, there was a noble knightly class and a slave class. Akin to the Vikings, the nobles were men of action, poised for aggression, conquest, and adventure. For an Achilles or an Agamemnon, *good* was equivalent to what the noble class cherished—pride, bravery, openness. This warrior aristocracy defined what was good as what they liked. That's all there was to it.

Yet, among the upper-crust tough guys there existed a priest class, who lacked the taste and temperament for steel and blood, but were hardly deficient in their desire to express what Nietzsche anointed their "will to power." Without moral connotations, the elites considered the laboring class as subhuman, as "the unlucky ones." And as the unfortunates who perhaps had to cart huge boulders to build the Coliseum, they resented their suffering. Brimming with thirst for power, the priestly class tapped into this *ressentiment*, eventually turning suffering and self-denial—what Nietzsche tabbed the "ascetic ideal"—into the touchstone for all virtues. Though it was in part a result of the spell cast by priestly purification rites, Nietzsche's account is murky as to the precise method by which this inversion of values took place; nevertheless, after the slave revolt, seeking glory or your own interests was a cause for consternation. If you wanted something for yourself, you needed to dress up that objective, both for yourself and others, as though it were only for the good of the community; for example, I want to go to medical school, not because I like the respect and salaries that doctors enjoy but because I want so badly to help people. Over time, and with a subtle form of psychological jujitsu, the priest class was able to hypnotize their warrior brethren into seeing themselves through a new set of categories, through the eyes of the enslaved and the ascetic ideal.

Harken to the Sermon on the Mount: "Blessed are the meek, for they shall inherit the earth." After the slave revolt, qualities formerly regarded as vices, like meekness, were magically transmogrified into signs of blessedness. If pride were not a sin, the timorous individual too cowardly to seek revenge could now be proud of turning the other cheek. Expressions of strength, ambition, and the craving for glory became suspect and were denounced as sinful.

As Nietzsche's genealogy has it, Judeo-Christianity was both the tool and the epitome of *ressentiment*. Nietzsche claimed the faith of Abraham and the crucifixion were an underhanded power grab: the weak mantled themselves with the authority to judge and laud it over others, to burn people at the stake, and consign them to the eternal punishment of hell. The end product of four generations of pastors, Nietzsche, whom his schoolmates once nicknamed "the Little Pastor," had a masterful command of the Bible and the writings of the church fathers. As if to reveal the ugly underbelly of the so-called religion of love, Nietzsche asks, "For *what* is it that constitutes the bliss of this Paradise, this paradise that Christians are climbing all over each other to reach?" Nietzsche answers, "We might even guess, but it is better to have it expressly described for us by an authority . . . Thomas Aquinas, the great teacher and saint. *Beati in regno coelesti*, he says, meek as a lamb, *videbunt poenas damnatorum, **ut beatitude illis magis complaceat**.*" In translation, "In order that the bliss of the saints may be more delightful for them and they may render more copious thanks to God for it, it is given to them to see perfectly the punishment of the damned."[5] Nietzsche adds a longer and more graphic expression from Tertullian, which strikes the same malicious chord that heaven would not be heaven unless the elect were able to tune in to the suffering of the damned at will. Christians who want to take a purifying lesson from Nietzsche might think in terms of trying to be honest enough with themselves about their less-than-holy impulses, on the aggressive and power motives that, like mites, can burrow their way into our postures of faith.

The desideratum of Nietzsche's genealogy of morals is

a "trans-valuation of values." Members of the philosophy guild celebrate their ability to ask foundational questions, but those queries are often nothing but prinked-up intellectual rebuses. Nietzsche, the philosopher with the hammer, banged out his own unhinging question: What is the value of our values? Or again, are our values adding value to our lives, or are they making us sickly? The ancient skeptics taught that when we have a question of truth or falsity, we first need a criterion to resolve the issue. Then arises the question that spurs skepticism. Whence comes the criterion? And what criterion did we use to arrive at it? To the point at hand, what is the criterion that Nietzsche uses to make his momentous assessment of the value of values?

Nietzsche declares that the grand moral theories of most philosophers are essentially self-portraits. The pre-Socratic philosopher Xenophanes taught that if horses had gods, their gods would look like horses, and Nietzsche continued Xenophanes's tradition of characterizing philosophers as masters of projection. Aristotle was the epitome of contemplation, and so when it came to illuminating the best life, it was of course one of contemplation. Kierkegaard was passion incarnate, and, not surprisingly, for him passion was the sine qua non of a life worth living. A sickly individual, Nietzsche had an ideal self that was an extrapolation from the desire for health and vigor that always escaped him. A shooting star of an academic, at a mere twenty-four Nietzsche was hired as a professor at the University of Basel, without having even defended his dissertation, but because of chronic migraines and other maladies he was forced to retire only a few years later. Having departed from the lecture hall, Nietzsche became an itinerant, moving from place to place, tirelessly seeking a sunny locale that would energize him, a place, usually in his beloved Italy, where he could breathe freely and create. Thus, health was the god term for Nietzsche and the scale for his reevaluation of values.

Nietzsche's notion of health was not limited to healthy digestion, strong lungs, and sinews. Health amounts to much more than its individual parts. To be healthy is to be brave, bold, and creative. It is to be a "free spirit," to be one who stands apart from the crowd and creates his or her own values. Napoleon and Goethe were exemplars, as was Jesus in his own way. Behold Nietzsche's portrait: "Such men," Nietzsche writes, "live in their own solar system—one has to look for them there." Such a self-defining man "is a star without an atmosphere. His eye, directed blazingly inward, looks outward, for appearance's sake only, extinct and icy. All around him, immediately upon the citadel of his pride beat the waves of folly and perversity; with loathing he turns away from them."[6]

Like most intellectual immortals, Nietzsche had a capacity to tolerate cognitive dissonance. An atheist of the fundamentalist stripe, he nevertheless recognized the genius of select true believers. He was also quick to admit that for all of its flaws and follies, the slave revolt produced an inner world.

Those disinclined to adventures and conquest now sought and produced adventures within themselves. As Nietzsche phrased it, "for the first time man became an interesting creature," and some of these interesting, inwardly turned creatures created divine works of art, like Dostoyevsky's *Brothers Karamazov* or *Notes from Underground*, the satirical novel that Nietzsche relished and helped shape his *On the Genealogy of Morals*.

Still, on balance, Nietzsche judged the slave revolt and slave morality, which he associated with democratic values, as putting us on a path to nihilism, to a herd state of mind that knew only two poles and two concerns, business and pleasure, work and play. At the end of the nineteenth century, Nietzsche described humanity as slipping toward a weariness that, à la "the last man," aches for nothing more than "pitiable comfortableness"—a pair of slippers, a flat-screen television, and some action movies. As culture became more civilized and bureaucratized, you could even hear the same grievances from none other than the hyper-rational protofeminist J. S. Mill:

> There has crept over the refined classes, over the whole
> class of gentleman in England . . . an inaptitude for
> every kind of struggle. This torpidity . . . is new in the
> world: but . . . it is a natural consequence of the prog-
> ress of civilization.[7]

Whereas we used to fantasize about everlasting fame, Nietzsche regarded today's everyman and everywoman as slouching toward becoming the bourgeois Babbitt whom, in contrast to his Superman or *Übermensch*, he baptized "The Last Man." The slave revolt leveled the prospects for greatness, looked askance at the heroic, and on Nietzsche's reckoning hampered the emergence of individuals powerful and creative enough to become a lodestar for humanity and our self-understanding. Nietzsche is open to criticism for valuing individual greatness and competition over what he surely would have judged to be the tepid ideal of cooperation. Even so, perhaps there is something to be learned from our Zarathustra.

What moral insight might we glean from the bespectacled, well-dressed, well-mannered scholar who would turn our moral sensibilities inside out? Lyrical philosopher that he was, Nietzsche felt free to take poetic license, sometimes to the point of verging on self-contradiction. However, aspects of moral counsel are easily extracted from the writer: Be courageous and creative.

Today, it is rare to hear someone make such an invocation. More than likely, those in earshot of such an appeal will interpret it as an accusation of weakness. For a trifling example, in this anxious and credential-crazed society, I have had students shuffle into my office holding back tears because they received a B-plus on a quiz instead of an A. At exam time, it seems like half my students are shaking in their boots, while another smaller portion of the class tries to deal with their anxiety by striking pirate poses of indifference. Last spring, our finals period fell close to the anniversary of the Normandy invasion. In the session before our exam, I was getting peppered with irritating probes about what was going to be on the test. Finally, like the Patton of the philosophy department, I all but shouted, "Get a grip!" Then I went on to remind my class of nineteen- and twenty-year-olds that, in June 1944, on the eve of D-day, General Eisenhower emerged from headquarters to have a somber talk with his troops. He spoke of the momentous importance of what they were about to undertake, but also warned that many of them would not be coming back. "There," I hectored, "was something to quake about." My halftime-like speech inspired a few of my charges to gather their strength, but others sneered and shook their heads at me disapprovingly, as though I were a remnant of the old order, an order that failed to recognize that test anxiety is a medical problem.

Lyrical philosopher that he was, Nietzsche felt free to take poetic license, sometimes to the point of verging on self-contradiction. However, aspects of moral counsel are easily extracted from the writer: Be courageous and creative.

In myriad ways, Nietzsche emphasizes the urgent importance of being able to get into the ring with your fears. After all, if you can't take a hit, much less absorb the fear of taking a hit, then there is no way around it: you are going to be morally challenged. Rather than shying away from our personal bogeymen, Nietzsche bids us to embrace the trials that tempt us to call in sick, because they are the pathway to becoming who we are.

I am reluctant to use another example from the world of the ring, but one of the reasons I have been training fighters for thirty years and counting is on account of lessons drawn from Aristotle and Nietzsche. Both taught that character is sculpted by how we cope with our fears. It would be a mistake to equate physical and moral courage; just the same, in a tight situation, if I had to choose, I would partner up with the person who had experience putting him- or herself at risk.

Everyone, or almost everyone, craves their red badge of courage. The most famous philosopher of nineteenth-century

---

In myriad ways, Nietzsche emphasizes the urgent importance of being able to get into the ring with your fears. Rather than shying away from our personal bogeymen, Nietzsche bids us to embrace the trials that tempt us to call in sick, because they are the pathway to becoming who we are.

Europe, G. W. F. Hegel (1770–1831) helps to explain why. In his famous allegory of the Lord and Bondsman, Hegel speculates that it is in mortal combat and ultimately in our willingness to give up our lives that we rise to a higher level of freedom and consciousness. If Hegel is correct, the lofty image that the warrior occupies in our society has something to do with the fact that in her willingness to sacrifice her own life, she has escaped the otherwise universal choke hold of death anxiety. The boxing ring is not the battlefield by any stretch of the imagination, but the fight game can be legitimately understood as a stylized version of Hegel's proverbial trial by battle; as such, it affords new possibilities of freedom and selfhood.

Today, the young and the privileged get very little practice in sparring with their angst. Maybe they should take up the sweet science. In a well-supervised boxing gym, athletes get regular workshops in handling their fears. I have one Nietzschean exercise that I call "the courage drill." One of the most difficult skills for an individual with pugilistic ambitions to master is staying in the pocket; that is, remaining within striking distance of his or her opponent. When your dance partner in violence launches his or her power punch, there is a natural instinct to retreat straight back, which both puts you on the nasty end of your rival's blow and leaves you out of position to counterpunch. With this exercise, I have one boxer shoot a combination, and I stand behind the person on defense so that he or she cannot step out of the pocket. When they fall back I don't hesitate to scold, "Come on, be brave!" And if my boxer happens to be one of my philosophy students, I might even add a snarky Nietzschean invocation, "Come on—live dangerously!"

Most philosophers bid us to go to war against our instincts. Socrates, for one, acts as though he can't wait to die in order to be unshackled from his body and the desires the flesh gives rise to. For Kant, moral worth has everything to do with overriding our inclinations. Again, Schopenhauer believed that the aim of life should be to slough off the will to live. In contrast, Nietzsche tries to reunite us with our instincts, no matter how base or unshaven they prove to be. One of Nietzsche's gripes about Christianity, the old moralists, and the ascetic idea was that they inculcated a distrust of anything that smacked of the ecstatic or, as he termed it, the "Dionysian." It is an ice cube down the back, but Nietzsche insists that there was a healthier time when we took unadulterated joy in watching the suffering of others. Hard to fathom? It shouldn't be.

Over the course of a lifetime, many of us glue ourselves to screens and gobble up thousands of graphic throat-slitting movies. Hollywood gift wraps our bloodlettings in morality tales, like a heroic serial killer who, working outside the law, kills evil serial killers! The cruelty we savor has to be on an HD screen and with a patina of justification. If you are going to blast people away, it has to be for the good of humankind. And yet, having enjoyed all the Hollywood gore, we rub our palms together and tell ourselves that there is nothing more abhorrent than violence and senseless suffering.

In the opening pages of *On the Genealogy of Morals*, Nietzsche expresses the hope that the breed of investigators he is trying to engender will "know how to keep their hearts as well as their sufferings in bounds and have trained themselves to sacrifice all desirability to truth." And then he finishes with "*every* truth, even plain, harsh, ugly, repellant, unchristian, immoral truth.—For such truths do exist."[8] There are many, but one of the ugly historical truths that Nietzsche claims to have cornered is this: "it is not long since princely weddings and public festivals of the more magnificent kind were unthinkable without executions, torturings, or perhaps an auto-da-fé."[9] Nietzsche contends that civilization, the process by which human beings were, so to speak, "tamed" and rendered predictable, was based on an ocean of blood. Consider Shakespeare's *The Merchant of Venice*, a testimony to an era when bad debts and broken promises were balanced out by the offended party being allowed to delight in the physical suffering imposed on the guilty culprit. Nietzsche wanted us to own a side of ourselves that we lock in the basement. He all but preaches that we need to be candid with ourselves about what we actually find appealing as opposed to what we would like to think we like.

Nietzsche had a discerning eye for the toxic feelings of suspicion, envy, and disguised ire. Again, I know where Nietzsche is calling from. Once upon a time, I was asked to do a taped interview on a radio show that regularly attracts over a million listeners. Weeks and months passed by and my interview was never aired. I made inquiries. Finally, the producer emailed me to say the interview did not hang together and that she could not broadcast the discussion on her show. I complained, at which point she had an underling inform me that putting my interview on the airwaves might damage my reputation. Naturally, I feigned indifference, but inwardly I was fuming and could not forgive the slight. This was three years ago, and sometimes, even now, when I can't sleep, I fantasize about how I might exact revenge: human, all too human. Father Nietzsche would understand my desire to repay this insult.

These days there is a robust industry of forgiveness experts, much of it orbiting around the idea that we need to be able to forgive ourselves, as though I had the authority to forgive myself for someone whom I have victimized! I might as well pretend that as a third party I could forgive the fiend who mugged and robbed my friend. Nietzsche does not prescribe self-forgiveness but something even more radical. Healthy consciousness requires forgetfulness. As Nietzsche describes it, you don't need to be able to forgive; you need to be able to forget both the transgressions of others and your own missteps. The coda to section 10 of the First Essay, Book 1, of *On the Genealogy of Morals* reads:

> To be incapable of taking one's enemies, one's accidents, even one's misdeeds for very long—that is the sign of strong full natures in whom there is an excess of power to form, to mold, to recuperate and to forget (a good example of this in modern times is Mirabeau, who had no memory for insults and vile actions done him and was unable to forgive simply because he—forgot). Such a man shakes off with a *single* shrug many vermin that eat deep into others; here alone genuine "love of one's enemies" is possible—supposing it to be possible at all on earth."[10]

While most philosophers praise memory and disparage forgetfulness, Nietzsche sees it the other way around. Forgetfulness is a form of spiritual digestion essential to spiritual well-being. We need to resist becoming moral stamp collectors. We need to be strong enough to let things go.

There is much that divides and unites Kierkegaard and Nietzsche. On a purely personal and psychological level, both had the ability to hold the wire of continuous hyperintense levels of intellectual stimulation that would have been more than enough to drive others to madness. For the most blatant of contrasts, Kierkegaard's life and works were

As Nietzsche describes it, you don't need to be able to forgive; you need to be able to forget both the transgressions of others and your own missteps.

faceted to the issue of faith. Stressing the striving aspect, Kierkegaard always described himself as becoming a Christian. He would have concurred with Nietzsche that faith in God is not exactly blessed by reason and that the faithful are only able to trust in God by power of the absurd. Like Nietzsche, Kierkegaard was a free spirit who found the cleverness and relentless, narrow-minded pragmatism of bourgeoisie society repugnant.

A couple of years before Nietzsche drifted into his decade of insanity, the Danish literary critic Georg Brandes introduced Nietzsche to Kierkegaard's writings. Though it is not clear how much of Kierkegaard he absorbed, philosopher Thomas Miles makes a strong case that Nietzsche read and was impacted by Kierkegaard's virulent *Attack upon "Christendom."* At bottom, both men were apostles of self-honesty, courage, and boundless passion.

Affinities aside, Nietzsche surely would have diagnosed Kierkegaard as having imbibed the poison of the slave revolt. Of "the man of *ressentiment*," the individual who is the end product of the slave revolt, Nietzsche says his "soul *squints*;

his spirit loves hiding places, secret paths and back doors, everything covert entices him as *his* world." An author who invites us to explore all the nooks and crannies of our inner lives, Kierkegaard would certainly have been counted a soul squinter. For a familiar example, remember Kierkegaard claims that happiness is despair's greatest hiding place. Nietzsche would have had a belly laugh or perhaps wretched at the idea that we ought to have third thoughts about those rare moments when we feel joyful and at home in ourselves.

Kierkegaard was also a priest of the Nietzsche-detested "ascetic ideal," an ideal demanding that the "purity of heart is to will one thing"—namely, what God wills. This ideal prescribes that wherever there is the natural desire to accrue some benefit for our actions or perhaps for a degree of reciprocity, then the heart is divided and ignoble. More than a dozen times, Kierkegaard reminds us that to become who you are, namely, a child of God, you must "die to this world," an age-old notion that would have given Nietzsche another of his debilitating migraines.

Kierkegaard's views on ethics were usually entwined with his endless reflections on faith. The question of whether or not something was ethical was seldom isolated from the issue of it's being an act of faith. No matter, Kierkegaard still manages to frame glimmering thoughts about the moral life. After all, he generated a veritable library of up-building literature, much of which could well be interpreted as moral self-help.

We have touched on this before but Kierkegaard believed the knowledge of right and wrong were universally distributed. Moral improvement is not a matter of acquiring more knowledge or skills of analysis. If it were, the economically/educationally disadvantaged would also be morally disadvantaged—and that would belie an unjust and immoral universe. Because Kierkegaard did not believe that the task of offering ethico-religious instruction was one of transmitting knowledge, he reconsidered what it meant and how to go about communicating the truths that matter, the truths that are a way of life. With ethics, there is no longer an object of knowledge to be passed along; instead, ethico-religious communication is primarily a matter of enlivening a person's relationship to their ideas. When we are faced with examples of moral greatness, for instance, we should not imagine that a Mandela or a Bonhoeffer is cut from a different cloth. Here, Kierkegaard would link arms with Sartre. Our moral capacities are not like athletic abilities. There is no such thing as a moral genius. Rather than passively admiring moral heroes, I ought to strive to follow their lead.

Again, Kierkegaard wrote thousands of pages of uplifting literature, spiritual and moral self-help. For Kierkegaard, part of what it means to build someone up is to nudge him or her out of an objective posture and cultivate in that individual a concern about what kind of person he or she is becoming. Students always come to me understandably absorbed in the question of vocation and what to do after college, but they seldom spend their time and energy thinking about what kind of human being they want to become.

Our moral capacities are not like athletic abilities. There is no such thing as a moral genius. Rather than passively admiring moral heroes, I ought to strive to follow their lead.

Early in his career, Kierkegaard drafted a series of lectures on indirect communication. Perhaps because he detected a contradiction in directly communicating about indirect communication, Kierkegaard never delivered or published these lectures. He left them in his notebooks, which he, in turn, left to posterity. In these notes, Kierkegaard asserted that moral education had more to do with drawing the truth out of a person than injecting them with it:

It may be that science can be pounded *into* a person, but as far as esthetic capability is concerned (simply because there is no object) and even more so with the ethical (simply because here in the strictest sense of the word there is no object), one has to pound it *out* of him. The corporal sees the soldier . . . in the farm boy and therefore says: I will have to pound the soldier out of him.[11]

On my reading, part of the "beating out" that Kierkegaard was prescribing consists of helping one another to avoid self-deception. In *The Sickness unto Death* Kierkegaard defines despair as an imbalance in the self. In the next section, he defines it in terms of different levels of consciousness of being a self. Finally, he begins part two with the simple decree, "Despair is sin." He then presses, *What is sin?*

For Kierkegaard, part of what it means to build someone up is to nudge him or her out of an objective posture and cultivate in that individual a concern about what kind of person he or she is becoming.

Kierkegaard's beloved Socrates held that sin is ignorance. But we can't be culpable if we are justifiably ignorant. For example, if you hand me a drink at a party unaware that it has been spiked with arsenic, you cannot be blamed, because you had no way of knowing. On the other hand, suppose we suffer and make others suffer from an ignorance that we have brought upon ourselves. Kierkegaard frequently presses us to understand that there are two ways of understanding: theoretical and practical. You can see him chuckling as he writes:

> It is exceedingly comic that a speaker with sincere voice and gestures, deeply stirred and deeply stirring, can movingly depict the truth, can face all the powers of evil and of hell boldly, with cool self-assurance in his bearing . . . it is exceedingly comic that almost simultaneously . . . he can timidly and cravenly cut and run away from the slightest inconvenience.[12]

A few pages later, in a brilliant paragraph that needs to be cited in full, Kierkegaard offers this vivid image of what happens when moral push comes to shove:

> In the life of the spirit there is no standing still . . . therefore if a person does not do what is right at the very second he knows it—then knowing simmers down. Next comes the question of how willing appraises what is known. Willing is dialectical and has under it the entire lower nature of man. If willing does not agree with what is known, then it does not necessarily follow that willing goes ahead and does the opposite of what knowing understood (presumably such strong opposites are rare); rather, willing allows some time to elapse, an interim called: "We shall look at it tomorrow." During all this, knowing becomes

more and more obscure, and the lower nature gains the upper hand more and more; alas, for the good must be done immediately, as soon as it is known, . . . but the lower nature's power lies in stretching things out. Gradually, willing's objections to this development lessen; it almost appears to be in collusion. And when knowing has become duly obscured, knowing and willing can better understand each other; eventually they agree completely, for now knowing has come over to the side of willing and admits that what it wants is absolutely right.[13]

The author draws a breath and concludes:

And this is how perhaps the great majority of men live: they work gradually at eclipsing their ethical and ethical-religious comprehension, which would lead them out into decisions and conclusions that their lower nature does not much care for, but they expand their esthetic and metaphysical comprehension, which ethically is a diversion.[14]

This passage had been critiqued for seeming to suggest that when it comes to moral decisions, we should go with whatever our gut tells us. But twice Kierkegaard indicates that it is not a matter of acting on impulse. Instead, we should act as soon as *we know* what the right thing to do is;

this *knowing* may or may not require intellectual consideration.

Imagine a moral decision that promises to deliver a large package of pain. Perhaps you are a police officer who has witnessed your friend and partner abusing a suspect. If you report your popular and well-respected colleague, you can be sure of quickly becoming a pariah in the department. As your commanding officer walks by and greets you, you momentarily consider saying something, but then the thought occurs that you have a family to support, and, besides, chances are no important change will come of you speaking up. Then you recall the case in 2017 of the Baltimore police officer who was poised to testify against his department. The day before his court date, he was mysteriously gunned down. Just a coincidence? The men and women in blue stick together. You decide this is too momentous a choice to make on the spot, so you say to yourself, "I will sleep on the decision." Kierkegaard's passage warns of the moral and spiritual perils of procrastination. The more time you put between yourself and an action, the more likely you are to convince yourself that the right thing to do is the easy thing to do.

I don't need to engage imagination to bring Kierkegaard's analysis to life. Memory will suffice. Years ago, I was taking a coaching certification clinic. Everyone was looking at each other's papers, conferring, and chuckling about the process, including the proctor, who was also a coach. I suppose we were all telling ourselves that we were sussed and seasoned coaches and that the information we were being examined on was useless. For the most part, that was true; nevertheless, we were always lecturing our athletes about being upstanding men and women of integrity. For a moment, I considered making a protest about the cheating. As it often happens with moral dilemmas, it was a situation that seemed to bubble up out of nowhere. Because of my need for affiliation, it felt like high stakes for me. Though it wasn't a life or death matter, I had recently been accepted into this fraternity and the last thing I wanted to do was stand up and start giving these veterans of the ring a moral lecture. Instead, I reassured myself that my colleagues and I were all knowledgeable and dedicated trainers generously volunteering our time to enrich the lives of young people, many of whom were at risk. I shouldn't have, but I kept my mouth shut, traded answers, joked around, and tried to forget what I didn't do.

Morally speaking, the temptation is not just to take the path of least resistance but to convince ourselves that the path of least resistance is the righteous path. As we continue to undermine our own sense of agency, our moral comprehension diminishes bit by bit. Because of this dynamic—or, as Kierkegaard might say, "dialectic"—we older folks sometimes look condescendingly at young people, thinking and perhaps muttering, "You're full of idealism, but in time you will learn." Learn what? How to shut down? That when you learn what life is all about you will darken your moral understanding by slowly talking yourselves out of truths that might earn you a cold shoulder or nix a promotion? Careerism, the comfort and sense of belonging that success yields, provides one of the most powerful impetuses for convincing ourselves to look the other way when a sacrifice is demanded.

Morally speaking, the temptation is not just to take the path of least resistance but to convince ourselves that the path of least resistance is the righteous path.

I should know.

In the 1980s, I needed to go to Denmark to learn Danish and finish my dissertation on Kierkegaard. I applied for a Fulbright and was excited to earn a spot on the list of finalists. At the time, there was a civil war going on in Nicaragua between the US-supported Contras and the Sandinistas. A close friend of mine, who was working in Nicaragua as a nurse, confided that the Contras were murdering doctors and medical personnel because they did not want the Sandinistas to gain popularity with the peasants. It deeply disturbed me that my government and taxes were supporting these killers, so I resolved, or rather "almost" resolved, to stop paying my taxes as a form of protest. One afternoon, a knowledgeable friend casually informed me that since the

Fulbright came through the State Department and the US government reacted negatively to tax resisting, I ought to reconsider protesting that way. Think again I did. À la Sartre's example, I even discussed the issue with a psychoanalyst who conveniently reassured me that it was grandiose of me to imagine that I, one person, a graduate student, could make a difference. Having let the issue percolate for a few days, I told myself the tired tale that I would have more of an impact after I took my doctorate. I wrote the check and sent my taxes in, and off I went to Denmark. I should and could have done otherwise. But maybe with its lack of consequences, that moment of regret is all too easy.

For the umpteenth time, "The self is a relation that relates itself to itself." Once more, there are different aspects of ourselves that we have to relate to one another, for example, our temporal and eternal dimensions. We are also burdened with having to relate ourselves to our past and future. Sweet days gone by are seldom an issue, but how to interpret major missteps that might prompt a person to lose faith in himself is a challenge that molds who we are.

Some thinkers have portrayed regret as a humanizing emotion. The twentieth-century moral philosopher Bernard Williams indicated that in instances where a person hurts another through no fault of her own (a truck driver who runs over a child, to use his example), we still expect her to feel remorseful, to feel the weight of the event more intensely than any spectator. "Other people," Williams writes, will try to comfort her, "but it is important that this is seen as something that should need to be done. Indeed, some doubt would be felt about a driver who too blandly or is too readily moved to that position of comfort."

Some hold the commonsense view that regret over a past event you can do nothing about is a waste of time when you can actually *do* something instead.

Spinoza reasoned that remorse and repentance are pernicious intoxicants that interfere with our understanding: It is out of rashness that we transgress, and it is out of rashness that we pound our heads about our transgressions. Our main aim, he believed, should be to avoid acting on impulse and emotion and to be guided by reason. Nietzsche agreed, saying remorse is a case of "adding to the first act of stupidity a second."

Regrets come in different forms. There are the faux pas and botched career moves. Just before he tumbled over the falls and out of existence, I asked an uncle if he had any regrets. His brow furrowed. He drew a deep breath as though what he was about to say was hard going. Then he confessed that the one thing he deeply regretted was selling a certain piece of property at a price that was much too low. That was it?

Last year, I was sitting deckside in Florida with a retiree who was beaming with friendliness as he bounced up and down in the pool. We started chatting, first about his hometown of Pittsburgh and the many great athletes who hailed from the City of Bridges. Somehow the conversation veered to Vietnam and his experiences there as a draftee. Embarrassed because I was spared from that jungle crucible, I just listened. First it was a few madcap stories about his arrival in 'Nam, but then his thoughts swam along a darker current. Moving his arms underwater, he recalled: "One time I had just gotten paid and I was gambling, playing poker with this fourteen-year-old Vietnamese kid. A great kid. He was studying English—wanted to make something of himself! Well, he won fair and square. He cleaned me out of my whole paycheck. I was drinking heavily back then. I picked up my M16, pointed it at him, and demanded my money back. He gave me my money." All I could do was gently smile and tell him (though it wasn't entirely true) that every ugly deed that I committed had also been fueled by alcohol. As though I'd missed the point, he responded, "I haven't had a drink in decades. But you know I'd give anything to be able to see that kid now grown." His voice cracked with emotion. "I would get on my knees and ask his forgiveness. I would say that I hope he has had a great life and that I am sorry." The otherwise jolly veteran-turned-accountant went on to hint that he had done worse things "over there." I hung my head and was thinking that maybe I should apologize to him for having been able and willing to get a deferment, ducking the harrowing machine that diced his sense of innocence.

Not long after, I found myself wide awake one night,

unable to sleep, when the incubus of a memory of another weak and selfish moment crawled out from under my bed. Sitting on my chest, it seemed to say, "O, teacher of ethics, how can you have any moral confidence in yourself after that?"

Moral regrets[15] are usually packed up in deep self-storage, and we often make a point of remembering to forget them, even while we are awash in pseudo-regrets. I often regale my male friends with the tale of the time during college football preseason when I started a fight with a coach on the practice field. This incident helped bring an end to my less-than-glorious gridiron career. In that sense, I regret it. But when I tell the story, it is always with a chuckle, as if to boast, "Wasn't I an outlaw in my day?"

As Freud and Kierkegaard taught, we always have to consider the affect, the mood with which an idea is expressed, in order to comprehend the meaning the idea has for us. The memory that the Vietnam vet bounced out of the pool was not of that backward boastful sort; it was a beach ball of sorrow. I suspect that he was a better person for having mulled over and hung his head for his behavior than he would have been had he resolved that what's done is done and never thought about it again.

In the chapter on faith I noted that for Kierkegaard, prayer does not change God—it changes, it develops, the person praying. Perhaps it is the same with regret. I can't rewind and expunge my past actions, but perhaps I change who I am in my act of remorse. "Make the most of your regrets," Henry David Thoreau advised, "never smother your sorrow, but tend and cherish it till it comes to have a separate and integral interest. To regret deeply is to live afresh."

To live afresh is to be morally born again.

For Kierkegaard, prayer does not change God—it changes, it develops, the person praying. Perhaps it is the same with regret. I can't rewind and expunge my past actions, but perhaps I change who I am in my act of remorse.

Clearly, considered in terms of moral development, this trio of existentialists offer a strange and diverse bit of moral instruction. Sartre urges us to recognize that our radical freedom breeds anxiety and that we have a proclivity to try to escape the angst in bad faith by denying our freedom. Nietzsche summons us to recognize that our moral values are not sacred and did not come from on high. If he were to offer a homily, it would include the suggestion that rather than torture ourselves and others, we ought to learn to let transgressions go and be attentive to emotions and power interests that stealthily infuse our moral sensibilities. Finally,

Kierkegaard instructs that the main obstacle to leading a righteous life is our predisposition to hoodwinking ourselves by talking ourselves out of doing the right thing when it requires sacrifices that diminish our happiness and satisfaction.

CHAPTER 7

LOVE

A few years ago, a dear friend of mine lost his wife. They had a long and tumultuous marriage. There were extended periods when my friend's wife was in such a fury, and with some reason, that she would barely speak to him. She developed what was judged to be a terminal form of cancer. She lost her enormous energy, lived in agony, and slumped into a deep and impenetrable funk. When she was going through chemotherapy my friend dutifully and lovingly spoon-fed and bathed her. An individual of considerable persuasive power, he exhorted her not to give up. Thanks to an experimental treatment, the cancer went into remission for a time but a couple of years later it raged back.

In the end, she contracted pneumonia and after a death-rattling few days, slipped into a coma-like state. My friend was bedside and had to give the order not to resuscitate.

Dealing with an emergency of my own, I could not attend the funeral in California. I called my pal of forty years and asked him how he felt. He sighed, hesitated a moment, and then he uttered the powerful and arresting truth, *"She knew me . . . and she loved me."* Not, "She knew me and *still* loved me." No, just, *"She knew me and loved me."*

How to give, find, and accept love? What do Kierkegaard and Dostoyevsky have to teach us on this triad of existential questions?

To be sure, there are different flavors of feelings that we call "love"—erotic, friendship, and familial. The Greeks distinguished between *eros* (erotic love), *agape* (selfless, sacrificial), and *philos* (friendship, brotherly love). With Kierkegaard, love, or rather the command to love, is central to what it means to be a Christian. Doubtless, the treatises on what Jesus meant by *love* could fill a floor of the Mall of America! And what about the people rushing about the Mall of America? What do they, what do we, think about love? Are the plethora of romantic comedies that we ingest any indication? Or Tinder and the matchmaking websites, many of which seem based on the premise that the search for a person to share your life with is akin to shopping for a car? We might as well have something like new car sticker sheets—Mr. or Ms. Lonelyheart is attractive, intelligent, friendly, enjoys skiing, wants to have children. You have some test drive dates and then . . . who knows? And what's wrong with that? I'm not sure. Maybe nothing.

How to give, find, and accept love? What do Kierkegaard and Dostoyevsky have to teach us on this triad of existential questions?

The existentialists were far from dewy-eyed about love. Some of these frequently sneering, wry characters outright deny the possibility that we can get outside of ourselves enough to love someone else. Not to include him among the Sartre and Camus cadre, but it was Luther's view that human beings are by nature "curved in" on themselves and as such we find it immensely difficult to break out of the lock of our own self-love. For Luther, this inwardly directed, selfish self-love was at the dark heart of our innate sinfulness. Today, we don't think in terms of an inward curve; instead we talk about a pandemic of narcissism, symptomized by the likes of selfies and self-promoting messages on Facebook.

To return to the existentialists, in Jean-Paul Sartre's play *No Exit*, written and produced during the Nazi occupation, a mysterious valet escorts three characters—Garcin, Inèz, and Estelle—into a room sparsely furnished in Second Empire style. Soon enough, they realize that they have died and gone to hell. They are dumbfounded by the lack of pincers and whips, but there is a less-than-obvious rack they are to be stretched on. During their lives on earth, each of them had culled their sense of themselves from the reactions of others. There is no mirror in their living room/cell. And just as they related to others when they had breath in their lungs, each of them treats their fellow denizens of hell as objects, as mirrors to see themselves in. Because they are all after the same self-affirmation, they can't look to their hellmates to secure their sense of identity. As the play closes, the murderer Garcin gets the idea and exclaims, "Hell is other people" because life is an endless struggle to establish yourself as a subject among others trying to do the same.

I have a tad of knowledge about the dynamic Sartre dramatized. In the mid-1980s, I used to drive a limo from Camden to Portland, Maine. Much like Newport, Rhode Island, Camden is a yachting town, popular with the fabulously wealthy. My job was to shuffle millionaires forty-five miles to the airport so they could catch their flights back to Palm Beach or wherever. One late night in the middle of the Maine woods, my Croesus of a client casually blurted out, "I am in the mood for a Mexican dinner and a margarita; can you find a place? Don't worry, I'll pay for your time." Because I had another ride waiting in Portland, I could not satisfy his whim. Used to using staff to get whatever he wanted, he pouted the rest of the way and then gave me a lousy tip. Being an airport limo driver was enough to turn me into Che Guevara. Most of my customers related to me as though I were an object, maybe a rudder on their sixty-foot sloop, or at least they treated me that way until I somehow managed to sneak in the fact that I had just received my doctorate from the University of Chicago. Then the tenor of the interactions usually, though not always, shifted. Then I was no longer a thing, or to use the existentialist Ralph Ellison's prescient words, I was no longer an "invisible man."

Like his friend Sartre, Camus had many romances but was not exactly a romantic on the topic of love. In his twenties, Camus published *The Stranger*. The bestseller made Camus an instant literary insider. Set in Algeria, the protagonist Meursault lives so close to his senses that he is almost reptilian in character. Like the writer who created him, Meursault savors the sun, the sea, swimming, and also romping in bed with a former officemate named Marie. One morning after sleeping together, Marie is clad in Meursault's pajamas. They are horsing around; Marie is giggling. Meursault recalls, "When she laughed I wanted her again. A minute later she asked me if I loved her. I told her it didn't mean anything but that I didn't think so. She looked sad."

In part one of the book, Meursault is not given to introspection. It is as though he believes we are just a beach for feelings to wash over us. Some feelings last longer than others, but they come and go and don't point to anything beyond themselves. One plausible interpretation is that Camus is intimating that the ideal of love is a Western bourgeois myth. If we were honest, we would admit that it is impossible to package and project our emotions into the future, as if to say I will feel about you in five, ten, or twenty years as I do now. Float that deflationary view of love and the frogs will start to croak about "what about commitment," but Meursault would shrug and ask what is commitment beyond promising to feign feelings after they have disappeared? Or perhaps, promising to act lovingly after the thrill is long gone.

In his personal life, Camus was a passionate romantic, but an unfaithful partner. His first marriage ended in divorce. Camus always complained that he believed marriage to be unnatural, but he tied the knot again in 1940, this time with the French pianist Francine Faure, who gave birth to twins. Camus had many dalliances, the most famous with the Spanish-born actress Maria Casares. Francine was so troubled by his infidelities that she attempted suicide. Camus's oblique confession of guilt is inscribed in *The Fall*, a mea culpa that ironically earned Camus the Nobel Prize for Literature in 1957, just three years before he was killed in a car crash.

Like his first literary success, *The Fall* is simply a portrait, or in this case a partial self-portrait, written in the form of an extended monologue. Though he bore another name earlier in life, the main character goes by the moniker Jean-Baptiste Clamence. Formally a fancy Parisian lawyer, Jean-Baptiste carries a business card that reads "Judge Penitent." As the novel unfolds, it becomes evident that this title is a caption on Baptiste's lascivious and egoistic behavior. One night, after enjoying a few hours between the sheets, Jean-Baptiste is walking home. He crosses a bridge and sees a titillating woman dressed in black. A second later she leaps from the bridge. Though he can hear her screams downstream, he does nothing, not even as much as reporting it to the police. Later in the text, Baptiste recalls that before the incident at the bridge, that is, the fall that is also his baptism, he might have boasted, "few creatures were more natural than I. I was altogether in harmony with life, fitting into it from top to bottom. . . . Life, its creatures and its gifts, offered themselves to me, and I accepted such marks of homage with a kindly pride. To tell the truth, just from being so fully and simply a man, I looked upon myself as something of a superman."[1] Back then, Baptiste defended the defenseless in court and helped the poor. After his awakening he realizes that even when he was engaged in ostensibly charitable works, he was always expressing his will to power, his will to be admired. As Luther might have put it, he was curved in on himself; it was always "I, I, I."

At one level, *The Fall* is a reflection on the problem of guilt in a world in which there is no longer any possibility of forgiveness. Baptiste plies his lawyerly trade with criminals in a seedy sector of Amsterdam. The Judge Penitent confesses that he only confesses his sins in order to escape judgment and perhaps to induce you, his listener, to reveal your own transgressions so he can turn the tables and pass judgment on you.

The Nietzschean gospel of Jean-Baptiste is that we are so driven by the need to be in power and to escape the judgment of others that we can't blast out of the circle of self-love. There are two characters sketched out in *The Fall* who might qualify as being capable of love, but to listen to Camus's creation, one in a billion people are up to it. Forget the Christian overtones—if love is caring about someone else as you care about yourself, how many of us can rise to the task? When fortune smiles on my friends, I effuse, "I'm so happy for you," but few and far between are the times when I can actually share in someone else's joy.

Again, Baptiste doesn't exactly conclude that love is impossible, but he comes close, saying, "Of course, true love is exceptional—two or three times a century, more or less. The rest of the time there is vanity and boredom."

As much as Camus, Sartre, and others moan about human beings, everyday people frequently lay down their lives for others, often strangers. Of course, cynics have a way of dismissing such acts of self-sacrifice. For the doubters, altruism is impossible; everything we do is motivated by self-interest. The doctor who leaves a comfy practice in Maine to serve the victims of the war in South Sudan has a selfish motive—maybe fear of guilt, maybe a desire to be a hero and become famous. Most of our actions come on the springs of a mélange of motives. You can always construct an explanation that seems to unmask the selfish aims be-hind supreme acts of love and self-sacrifice. Perhaps the most attractive aspect of the claim that there are no unselfish actions is that they conveniently free us from feeling duty bound to take a few steps along the same path. *Oh, I would like to help you but I'm afraid that if I did, I would only be trying to assuage my own sense of guilt. Therefore, sorry, you are on your own.*

But does true love really exist? You can't see it. On that basis, faithful members of the empiricist congregation might find themselves in company with Jean-Baptiste. And yet, as cited above, Kierkegaard has a cautionary word for those whose vision of life does not extend beyond their line of vision: "If it were so, as conceited sagacity, proud of not being deceived, thinks, that we should believe nothing that we cannot see with our physical eyes, then we first and foremost ought to give up believing in love."

From Kierkegaard's vantage point, the hardheaded, probability-calculating individual who talks himself out of love has talked himself out of that which is most precious in life. Kierkegaard admonishes: "To defraud oneself of love is the most terrible, is an eternal loss, for which there is no compensation either in time or eternity."

Sadly, on the face of it, Kierkegaard did just that—he de-frauded himself of love. In one of the most poignant philo-sophical love stories of all time, the twenty-seven-year-old magister broke off his thirteen-month engagement with

Regine Olsen, a horrendous scandal among the Copenhagen elite. Everyone, his own brother included, thought Søren was acting like a cruel cad. Regine's father, a lawyer, made a desperate personal appeal to him to reconsider, pleading that his distraught daughter was nearly suicidal. But Kierkegaard was unrelenting, despite the fact that in his journals he wrote long, complicated entries affirming that Regine was the wife of his eternal soul, that she was the only one for him.

From Kierkegaard's vantage point, the hardheaded, probability-calculating individual who talks himself out of love has talked himself out of that which is most precious in life.

What prompted him to make the break? He went back and forth, and round and round. In his daily notes to himself, Kierkegaard explained that he did not want to bring Regine into the profound depression that seemed to afflict all the men in his family; at other points, he intimated that it was his calling to be a religious author. Soon after he returned her ring, and hoping to help her break the tie that bound them together, Kierkegaard traveled to Berlin, where he wrote letters to his friend Emil Boesen, who was instructed to calmly circulate the fiction that Kierkegaard was sowing his wild oats. Nothing could have been further from the truth. With preternatural verve, he was attending lectures, writing his sprawling *Either/Or*, a raft of religious discourses, and beginning work on the classic *Fear and Trembling*.

A couple of years after the breakup, Regine recovered and married. Mortal that the literary immortal was, Kierkegaard was furious at the news. Still, he always retained his love for his former fiancée, sending her vellum copies of all his books. He even approached her husband, Fritz Schlegel, asking him if it might be possible that he reenter into a friendship with the now Fru Schlegel. The husband refused.

Of course, a therapist would have told Kierkegaard to move on. But Kierkegaard believed that once you declare someone to be your eternal love, you need to keep that love alive, to "keep the wound open." This, of course, rings highly neurotic to our ears, but perhaps that is because we misunderstand love.

By the end of his short life, Kierkegaard was estranged from his only surviving brother and most of his friends. So why should we turn to the man who became a veritable recluse for wisdom on love? Perhaps because the reason Kierkegaard was alien to everyone is that he loved his friends and fellow Danes enough to tell them what they would have preferred not to hear.

On the surface, this vignette will seem remote from the issue of love, but not so. One afternoon, when I was a graduate student, I floated into Professor Rieff's office, proudly announcing that an essay of mine had just been accepted for publication in a top-flight journal. "Well done," said Professor Rieff, and then he began chiding me, saying that I smelled like ambition and that if I wanted to be a writer I should go and be a writer rather than trying to secure a faculty position. Rieff lectured that most professors were too narcissistic to be the authority figures they needed to be. Rather than confront a student about his or her manners or intellectual progress, he told me, most academicians would prefer to keep things quiet so as to be left in peace to write their next forgettable article. Who needs the conflict?

Rieff practiced what he preached, telling me in no uncertain terms that, despite my impending scholarly publication, I wasn't progressing as much as he would have liked. He ended our meeting with a hand on my shoulder and a stern look in the eye, saying, "Gordon, if you really care about your students, you will tell them the messy truths, even if it makes them angry."

That is how I like to think the critic Kierkegaard regarded his relationship to Danish society. By expounding on his understanding of the New Testament, Kierkegaard reminds his increasingly secularized fellow Danes that they—and we—have been *commanded* by God to love. He hints that the notion of love as a *duty* is so alien to our natural way of thinking that it is unlikely that any human being could have ever come up with such a bizarre idea. It had to be God.

Works of Love is rife with observations that challenge our assumptions about love. For instance, Kierkegaard articulates the austere idea that preferential love, loving someone for the qualities they possess—a curvaceous figure, a razor-sharp intellect, wit, or whatever—or because they are blood related is at bottom an expression of self-love. You love them either as an extension of yourself or because they fulfill some deep-seated desires. Preferential love comes easy to anyone with even a dab of humanity. Murderous mobsters love their children and their pals. There is nothing special about being able to love and make sacrifices for people you identify with, like your children. Beyond pushing us to reevaluate some of the forms of love that come so naturally, much of *Works of Love* is devoted to, well, the works of love. According to Kierkegaard, one of these works is nothing other than the strange duty to *presuppose love* in others; that is, in opposition to Sartre, Camus, and Nietzsche, Kierkegaard believes that we are duty bound to presuppose an essential ability to love in everyone, not only in people we feel simpatico toward but also in those whom we cut across the street to avoid.

I have an inkling of what this work might be like. It was the first faculty meeting of the year, one that nearly everyone attends. I glanced up at a colleague with whom I have had some heated battles. *Hate* might be too strong a term; then again, maybe not. We have been fellow teachers for twenty years, but like high school kids, we don't say hello to each other when we cross paths. That day, when I saw my academic archenemy, I was suddenly wrapped in a waft of warmth and good will. Almost automatically, I smiled and my hand flashed up in a friendly wave. Shocked, my less than friend jerked his hand up in a return half-wave but then pulled his paw back and looked the other way. For a few ticks, the animus and dissimilarity between us vanished. It hit me that we were just two struggling and bumbling human beings.

According to Kierkegaard, one of these works is nothing other than the strange duty to *presuppose love* in others; that is, in opposition to Sartre, Camus, and Nietzsche, Kierkegaard believes that we are duty bound to presuppose an essential ability to love in everyone, not only in people we feel simpatico toward but also in those whom we cut across the street to avoid.

On Kierkegaard's reading, the injunction to love one another has everything to do with the fact that in God's eyes we are all equal. Kierkegaard writes:

Dissimilarity is temporality's method of confusing that marks every human being differently, but the neighbor is eternity's mark—on every human being. Take many sheets of paper, write something different on each one; then no one will be like another. But then again take each single sheet; do not let yourself be confused by the diverse inscriptions, hold it up to the light, and you will see a common watermark on all of them. In the same way the neighbor is the common watermark.[2]

As earlier noted, one sign of the fallenness of this world is our addiction to our differences. I have known students to land fellowships and get accepted to elite programs and soon enough they are eager to find out how many others were shut out at the door. The more that are rejected the better they feel about themselves. Kierkegaard maintained that we are so attached to comparisons and our differences that we take them into the cemetery, with the big shots getting large monuments and maybe even a small chain-link fence to keep the hoi polloi out of their eternal resting place. Kierkegaard professed that when it comes to the spiritual life and to love we see best when our eyes are tightly shut and we are blind to the differences between ourselves and our neighbor. Closing our lids illuminates the watermark of the only true equality, equality before God.

Kierkegaard would wryly smile that my experience at the faculty meeting was a passing mood, something that "happened to me." It was not a love grounded in a sense of duty. I suspect the reductionists would say the same, that I was experiencing some sort of neurochemical rainbow. The surge of fellow feeling was, in fact, so out of the ordinary that for a moment I wondered if something might be wrong, that maybe the sudden and strange feeling was an insight granted just before my lights were going out, a peek given to punish me with the thought—"this is the kind of person you could have been!" In the end, maybe it is best to think of such heart-opening moments as affective internal landmarks that we can remember and strive to climb back to.

One of the cavils that I have with Kierkegaard's otherwise rich, illuminating interpretation of love is that he may have given a cold shoulder to the feeling aspect of love. Kierkegaard describes love as a duty, a passion, a need, but tenderness is certainly not foremost in his analysis. Any account of love that excludes tenderness is lacking. Kant, the Socrates of the Enlightenment, contended that when Jesus commanded love, he could not have meant much more than being respectful and helpful to others because, *pace* Kant, love considered as a feeling can't be commanded. After all, you cannot will an emotion. To Kant's point, I may put on my boots and gloves and help my irascible neighbor shovel her snow, but I can't will myself to feel warmly toward the icy woman who scolds kids when they scamper across her yard. And yet, both the existentialists and the American pragmatists opined that we can do more than we might

think to nudge our emotions in directions we would like them to go.

If a primary aim in life is to develop into a caring and connected human being (admittedly a big if), rather than, say, thinking of oneself as a tourist collecting as many pleasant and fulfilling experiences as possible, then surely a capacity for loving feelings must play a role. Of course, that softening of the heart does not guarantee our humanity. After all, Hitler teared up over his pooch. Maybe Genghis Khan did the same over his horses. Still, an otherwise upright person who could walk by a little girl greeting her soldier dad coming home from war without heat coming to the cheeks is missing something. The person stopped in their tracks by the sight of a hunched, old woman, bags in hands, waiting in a thick snowfall to be picked up from a shopping trip might be in a better spiritual place than those of us marching with our heads down, consumed with the pressing problem of how we can get some work in after dinner and still catch the next episode of *Game of Thrones*.

Any account of love that excludes tenderness is lacking.

Most members of the Socrates guild, most who identify themselves as philosophers, begin inquiries with a search for a definition. But as previously noted, the perturbations of the inner world are difficult to speak readily about or distinguish from one another without the use of metaphors. The idea of tenderness usually calls to mind a softening of the inner self. The ancient Greeks, who understood psychological matters in terms of the elements, believed that too much Spartan tough-guy training literally desiccated the soul, rendering it hard and insensitive. For them, tenderness would have involved a moistening of the psyche and an opening up to the impingement of the outer world. When we say that an injury is tender, we mean that it is hypersensitive to the touch. In moments of tenderness, it is as though the ego and all its machinations momentarily melt away so that our feelings are heightened and we are moved by the impulse to reach out with a comforting hand.

For raw-edged instance a few years ago, my wife, Susan, and I were involved in a frightful car crash in the frozen tundra of the Minnesota countryside. After the collision, and looking down into her fluttering eyes, I held my emotions in check as the EMTs strapped her to a board for a helicopter ride to the trauma center in Minneapolis. But then I glanced at my twentysomething son, who had raced to the scene. I glimpsed his cheeks working with love and fear for his mom, as he tried to keep his inner universe intact. The sight of him undid me. In a tsunami of affection, all my stoicism and calm reason began to fly with the geese winging overhead.

When we say that an injury is tender, we mean that it is hypersensitive to the touch. In moments of tenderness, it is as though the ego and all its machinations momentarily melt away so that our feelings are heightened and we are moved by the impulse to reach out with a comforting hand.

The most famous philosophical meditation on love is Plato's *Symposium*. Few women populate the Platonic dialogues, but here Socrates attests that he absorbed his lessons on love from the priestess Diotima, who taught him that love is a cupid-like desire for the beautiful. All of us are steeped with an intuition that possessing the beautiful will ensure happiness. According to Diotima, we begin spellbound by the beauty of the physical form, then, if and when we mature, we are attracted first to the loveliness of the virtuous soul, and then to the beauty of laws that nurture souls.

My Diotima, Fyodor Dostoyevsky, brilliantly articulates the unexpected problem of accepting love. In *The Idiot*, an astounding portrait of Jesus, Dostoyevsky hints at the brow-raising position that facing the ultimate truth does not demand mental health but a pathological state of mind. More bluntly stated, you have to be crazy to handle the truth.

Dostoyevsky easily fulfilled his own requirement. He was highly neurotic, and given all that he endured, it is no wonder. He was born in Moscow in 1821. An engineer, Dostoyevsky served in the army. Afterward, he became involved with a group of idealists whose aim was to topple the Czar and democratize the Russian government. In 1849, the Czarist police arrested Dostoyevsky and other members of the group. After languishing in prison for months, Dostoyevsky and some of his comrades were taken by wagon, dressed in white cloth, tied to a stake, and asked to kiss the cross in preparation for execution. Just before they were to be shot, amid drum rolls, the execution was called off. His sentence was commuted to four years in prison in Siberia, followed by four years of military service.

After he was released from custody, Dostoyevsky's beloved brother Mikhail died, and he took on the financial responsibilities of his sibling's sizeable family. Dostoyevsky made his daily bread as an author, but because of his pressing financial responsibilities, he was always forced to sell the rights to future works at low rates just to make ends meet. He was severely epileptic, and just when the publishers were pounding at his door, he would often suffer a seizure that erased the memory of the plot he was constructing. As his second wife and secretary, Anna Grigoryevna Dostoyevsky, remembers, a few days before an installment was due and the creditors were about to start carting off the furniture,

Dostoyevsky would pace the floors of his apartment dictating the likes of what might be the greatest novel ever written, *The Brothers Karamazov.*

Given his horrific prison experiences, captured in *The House of the Dead,* the themes that occupied Dostoyevsky's real and imagined life were insults, humiliation, and moral self-degradation. In 1864, Dostoyevsky penned one of the nastiest satires in history, *Notes from Underground.* On reading the text, one Russian critic wrote a review, reasonably titled "A Cruel Talent." This novella is in part a rebuttal to Nikolay Chernyshevsky's *What Is to Be Done?* In his novel, the optimist reformer Chernyshevsky contends that with the right sociopolitical arrangements, human beings would cease eviscerating one another and live together in peace and harmony.

Dostoyevsky's novel is like the two books by Camus we have addressed, a parody in the form of a portrait. At one level, it is an argument that no amount of political, economic, or social engineering will deliver us from ourselves. On Dostoyevsky's reckoning, human beings are spiders, ungrateful bipeds who would prefer expressing their will to power even at the cost of their own happiness. You could read *Notes from Underground* as supporting the psychological thesis captured in the story of Genesis: If we were in Eden, we would follow Adam's lead and turn paradise upside down into an eventual Auschwitz.

Dostoyevsky's chief character is a former clerk who, through a meager inheritance, has just enough money to retire early. Socrates commanded, "Know thyself." Dostoyevsky and others in the existential tradition were taken up with the question of whether or not we can know ourselves without faith in God. The book is written from the narrator's standpoint of someone looking back across forty years. The Underground Man wants to see if he can be totally honest with himself. This project entails retrieving the memory of a choice that seems to have determined the course of his life.

Like tenderness, awkwardness is a theme that philosophers have placed in a forgotten file cabinet. Still, if you want to prepare someone for life, it would be good to remind them that life is replete with awkward situations: responding to friends who are deep in grief, bumping into people you have to pretend you are friends with when you have nothing to say to one another. Dostoyevsky is the Rembrandt and Mozart of those lip-twitching scenes. In part two of the novella, the Underground Man recollects forcing an invite to a send-off party for a rich army captain and former schoolmate named Zverkov. Much like Dostoyevsky himself, the Underground Man is umbrageous, always given to causing scenes. Though it is evident that no one wants him there, he manages to get himself included in the party. In a Freudian slip, one of the other celebrants tells him that the soiree is an hour earlier than it is. By the time the party arrives at the restaurant, the Underground Man is in a high dudgeon. After irritating the group with his snide and condescending remarks, everyone takes to ignoring him. He gets the hint, but out of stubbornness and spite the Underground Man refuses to excuse himself. Instead, he retreats to a nearby table, where he drinks himself into a besotted state and an emotional lather. Finally, when the party is about to disperse and the guests are offering tributes, our friend insists on making a toast in which he insults Zverkov, the guest of honor. A tissue of contradictions, the Underground Man tries to make amends. Zverkov interrupts and contemptuously replies that the Underground Man is a bug, too far beneath him to be taken seriously. "Insulted me?" says Zverkov. "You? In-sul-ted me? My dear sir, I want you to know that never, under any circumstances, could you possibly insult *me!*"

Far past midnight, the partiers rush off to a brothel. A virtuoso of self-humiliation, our antihero borrows money from a disdainful acquaintance and hires a sled to take him to the house of ill-repute, where he is intent on slapping Zverkov's face. By the time he arrives, however, the revelers have left and he is unable to slake his burning thirst for revenge. Still, a line of prostitutes wait in front of him, so he makes an arrangement with a girl named Liza. A couple of hours after having sex, he begins to work at his real thrill, toying with the young girl's mind. The Underground Man recalls:

My mind was in a daze. It was as though something were hanging over me, provoking, agitating, and disturbing me. . . . A dismal thought was conceived in my brain and spread throughout my whole body like a nasty sensation, such as one feels upon entering a damp, moldy underground cellar.[3]

A conversation begins. At first Liza responds mordantly to his expressions of interest and his tragic, half-made-up tale about the recent death and burial of another prostitute from a business down the street. Gradually, he gains Liza's trust with stories of the familial life she is depriving herself of. Surprised at his own feeling, the game continues. In a long-inspired speech, he calls Liza's father and mother to mind. In touching detail, the Underground Man describes the joys of motherhood that she will be missing out on, a baby breastfeeding, "the chubby, rosy little baby sprawls and snuggles; his little hands and feet are plump; his little nails are clean and tiny . . . his little eyes look as if he already understood everything. As he suckles, he tugs at your breast playfully."[4] Impassioned, the Underground Man prattles on. The Muse is with him; he gives the speech of his life.

Silence follows as he waits for Liza's response. One of the fears that the Underground Man harbors about himself is that he is a pretentious pate whose life is fashioned from novels. After listening to him, Liza stumbles a bit, then somewhat sarcastically blurts out that his tirade sounds like a book. Decades down the line, he recalls, "Her remark wounded me dreadfully. That's not what I expected. . . . 'Just you wait,' I thought." Revenge will be his.

The ideas are whips, but the writing is ethereal. As the sun begins to rise, the Underground Man prepares to leave. Impulsively, he scribbles his address down and invites Liza to visit him at his home, an invitation which he immediately knows is a mistake.

Four days later he is disgruntled and disheveled, embattled in a loud and ugly fray with his irksome housekeeper. There is a knock at the door. It's Liza. Our man is in a fury and wrapped in a dirty yellow bathrobe. No longer looking like a savior, he is frothing with ire at Liza for catching him in this compromised state. By sitting with her for five minutes without uttering a word, he makes the situation as tortuously uncomfortable as possible for her. Eventually, he boils over into a confession to Liza that he was just using her to vent his anger and slake his thirst for revenge. He hisses, "I'd been humiliated, and I wanted to humiliate someone else."[5]

Shaking, he continues: "The fact that I'd appeared to you then as such a hero, and that now you'd suddenly see me in this torn dressing gown, dilapidated and revolting. . . . By now surely even you've guessed that I'll never forgive you for having come upon me in this dressing gown."

Amazingly, Liza is not repulsed by the tirade. As he

weeps and rants, she recognizes him for the unhappy and angry man that he is. More than that, she knows that even though the Underground Man believes he was just playing with her, there were earnest feelings as well. She responds to his attack by putting her arms around his neck and crying with him. Sobbing, the Underground Man buries his head in the sofa. Then comes one of the most deliciously sinister passages in literature:

> But the trouble was that my hysterics had to end sometime. And so . . . lying there on the sofa and pressing my face firmly into that nasty leather cushion of mine, I began to sense gradually, distantly, involuntarily, but irresistibly, that it would be awkward for me to raise my head and look Liza straight in the eye. What was I ashamed of? I don't know, but I was ashamed . . . precisely because I felt too ashamed to look at her, that another feeling was suddenly kindled and burst into flame in my heart—the feeling of domination and possession. My eyes gleamed with passion; I pressed her hands tightly. How I hated her and felt drawn to her simultaneously![6]

The combination of attraction and repulsion echoes Kierkegaard's recipe for anxiety. The Underground Man cryptically cries out, "I want to be good but they won't let me." Part of him hungers for Liza's love, but he can't accept it because that would mean feeling as though he were on a lower plane. He bolts out of the room and leaves Liza sitting alone. Discomfiting minutes tick by with poor Liza sitting there in a daze. Finally, he taps on the screen indicating that she should leave. With a very sad countenance, she gathers up her things and says goodbye. A study in moral self-degradation, the Underground Man grabs her hand and places a five-ruble note in her palm.

Liza flies out the door into the snow-slanting late afternoon, gone forever. As usual, the Underground Man has third thoughts, calls to Liza, and dashes out after her, but she is gone, and so is his singular chance at real love. Back at his apartment, he espies the crumpled-up five-ruble note. This was the memory, the memory that haunted the Underground Man for forty years, and yet, even after that expanse of time, he fails to grasp that it was his pride that defrauded him of being able to accept love.

To return to the tale that began this chapter, for all their marital strife, in the end, my bereft widower friend was able to accept being loved as the imperfect human being he knew himself to be when the doors were closed and the shades drawn. Despite the pain he caused her, his wife loved him, not some idealized version of him.

Perhaps as a way of defending ourselves against our own doubts and inner voices, many of us hanker for admiration. We yearn to be desired, valued. We want to be loved as the people we aspire and perhaps imagine ourselves to be, not the flesh-and-blood fallible creatures that we are. Being loved for the sometimes kind and at other times tantrum-throwing child that we might be feels too much like pity, like forgiveness. Liza is, of course, a Christ-like figure, and one of the messages in this brutal book seems to be that pride impedes our ability to accept Christ's love and forgiveness. Both Nietzsche and Freud counted Dostoyevsky among the greatest psychologists in history. According to Dostoyevsky, if there is one thing that will drive a person to distraction, it is being forgiven. I know this to be true from both ends of the experience.

We want to be loved as the people we aspire and perhaps imagine ourselves to be, not the flesh-and-blood fallible creatures that we are. Being loved for the sometimes kind and at other times tantrum-throwing child that we might be feels too much like pity, like forgiveness.

When I was a boy, my father would come home from his club late, having had two too many martinis, and go on a rampage. Maybe I was six at the time. Up until then I had slumbered through my father's rants. One night I woke up to a new and terrifying reality of the house being torn apart. Back then, my dad was my buddy and hero. In between rounds of their battle, my mother came upstairs, wiped my tears away, and tried to comfort me, saying, "All daddies get drunk sometime." My mother didn't drink, and she wasn't one to back down from a fight. At a lull in the strife, I crept downstairs and up to my father. It was dark. I had never seen him look so disheveled. He put his hand on my head and said, "Get back to bed." I didn't move but softly said, "It's okay, all daddies get drunk sometime." In my own little boy way, I was saying, "I know you and love you." He pushed me across the room and I beat it back upstairs with a disappointment long in dissipating.

But I have shuffled in my father's shoes as well. A few years back, I started a loud and embarrassing squabble with my wife at my son's wedding reception. Up until that moment it had been a glorious day. Really, the perfect wedding. But beer, coupled with my overheated brain, brought a piece of me to the surface that had been submerged for decades. Before I knew it, I was red-faced and angrily screaming, enough that my other son had to pull me aside. The next day, I could not look myself in the mirror. At breakfast, one of my boys put his hand on my shoulder and out of nowhere quietly said, "Don't worry about last night, pops." I was silent for a moment, then hissed, "There is nothing I need to worry about, thank you." "All right," he said, withdrawing his palm from this Underground Man's shoulder and walking away.

My sons saw a side of me that I imagined had long ago vanished. I initially resented being seen soul naked. Nevertheless, I am many things but no Underground Man. A few minutes later, I came to my senses, threaded my arm around him, and, kid-like, rested my head on his shoulder—tearfully whispering, "I am so damn sorry."

Kierkegaard taught that Jesus's love commandment, namely, love thy neighbor as thyself, first and foremost requires proper self-love. This nonnarcissist caring relationship to the self is remote from the vanity and self-obsession that we tend to equate with self-love.

Over the course of my life, I have suffered through seemingly endless orgies of self-hatred. During those horrid spells, I would usually manage to go through the right motions, give due thanks and warm hugs to people who stood steadfastly by me. Nevertheless, I did not really appreciate or appropriate their love. In fact, as though they had been duped, I would often wonder, What is it with these people? Why would they want anything to do with me? For lack of proper self-love, the frothing fury in the furnace of my depression had me convinced that at heart and at bottom, I was a nasty Underground Man, and if the people around me only realized that, they would not be around me for very long.

Pardon the repeats and what rings of a sermon, but it is paradoxical: we need the love of others to love ourselves, but in order to be nurtured by the love of others, we need to love ourselves sufficiently to accept that love. Though it would take us far beyond the parameters of this chapter, herein lies part of the poison of racism and oppression. They profoundly damage a person's ability to love themselves.

Earlier in this chapter, I mined Kierkegaard's insight that the duty and work of love is *to presuppose love*—not just the love in others, but perhaps above all, the love in ourselves. Had he done that work, Dostoyevsky's Underground Man might have been able to let Liza hold and comfort him. He might have ceased being the Underground Man.

EPILOGUE

The reflections in the previous pages are gathered together under the rubric "survival guide." Still, this book is not a Baedeker on how to lead a happy or happier life. The assumption underlying these meditations is that, for all the jottings in your gratitude journal, leading an authentic life remains a Sisyphean labor. Author and self-proclaimed boozer Charles Bukowski titled one of his books *What Matters Most Is How Well You Walk Through the Fire*, not ". . . how well you walk through summer days romping on the beach with your kids."

As I mentioned in the introduction, I was attracted to the existentialists because, more than any other assemblage of authors, they recognized and addressed the hard fact that life is not a romantic journey but a daunting trek, or maybe, as Schopenhauer writes, "a task to be worked off." Still, the writers placed into conversation in this book are by no means in agreement with Schopenhauer's grievance that "the world is just *hell*, and in it, human beings are the tortured souls on the one hand and the devils on the other." Despite all his moans about and trenchant critiques of modernity, Camus tellingly confided, "in the midst of winter, I found there was, within me, an invincible summer." From Kierkegaard to Camus, the existentialists are profoundly aware that life is an incomparable gift, albeit a gift that is also a challenge.

When you are determined to take on a challenge, it is reasonable to register the impediments that might obstruct your efforts, whether this new challenge is learning a foreign language or starting a rigorous exercise program. Unblinkered, the existentialists took careful heed of life's many obstacles. Most of us would agree, for instance, that a loveless life is a lifeless life. But how many of us are similarly able to appreciate Dostoyevsky's insight that because we need to feel in control, accepting love for who we are (as opposed to wanting to be loved for our accomplishments or looks) is one of the most daunting stumbling blocks to true intimacy? Despite its limitations, this survival guide is designed to help you get over this and other stumbling blocks.

From Kierkegaard to Camus, the existentialists are profoundly aware that life is an incomparable gift, albeit a gift that is also a challenge.

And, yet, in his Seventh Letter, Plato questions if books are even a boon to wisdom. After all, three of history's greatest sages—Jesus, Buddha, and Socrates—did not leave us with any of their writings. Though he recognizes how the stylus aids memory, Plato seems dubious about the written word's ability to empower the good and just life. Plato reckoned that committing truths or, for that matter, arguments to memory was not enough. Kierkegaard, an ever-present voice in this book, agreed with Plato. He stood firm on the claim that if ideas are going to impress, they have to be appropriated, passionately, by the individual. Like sparrows in a barn, strings of pithy quotes flit in and out of the psyche. Maybe the same holds for a paraphrase. I am therefore reluctant to condense and repackage some of the existential nostrums that I have attempted to put on the counter in these pages.

Then again, I don't hesitate to recapitulate ideas in my role as a professor. In the final weeks of my ethics courses, I always work with students in assembling a list of potentially life-impacting insights garnered from the twenty or so thinkers we have been scratching our heads over throughout the semester.

For instance, we devote two full weeks to Aristotle, who contends that life is too complex to come up with a universal moral rule book to cover every situation. When unsure about the right course of action, Plato's prize pupil teaches, seek out and try to imitate a virtuous individual.

Problems, however, immediately arise; how, pray tell, is the person who has not yet achieved moral excellence supposed to identify the virtuous individual? In other words, there are problems with Aristotle's "virtue ethics," just as there are with every other ethical theory. Still, Aristotle serves up plenty of moral insights in his work. As previously discussed, it is not enough to know the good; one needs to possess the character to abide by that knowledge, which requires courage and the ability to deal with fear. The psychologist Aristotle avers that cultivating courage requires practicing with fear, which is why I mentioned boxing as a good place to get in some sparring with the jitters.

What is good for class, then, is also likely good for a book. So, despite my hesitance, perhaps there is value in distilling some of the most salient existential prescriptions in our survival guide.

One idea or perhaps presupposition that our reflections orbited around was the notion that we are self-conscious/self-relating creatures, creatures who might not always be conscious of the feelings informing the way we relate to ourselves but who nonetheless have some control over the way we relate to our inner lives. It is a truism to observe that we abide in a world that medicalizes inconvenient thoughts, moods, and emotions. This retrenchment may have helped destigmatize mental illness. Just the same, we tendered the idea in the chapter about anxiety that anxiety is not simply a disrupting affect accompanied by sweaty palms and an increased pulse rate. It is a feeling with a message, one with an important cognitive component.

Some recognize that a certain level of anxiety is helpful in sparking alertness, but our thinking on the previous pages went beyond that. Remember Kierkegaard's claim that to be anxious in the right way, about the right issues, is to learn the ultimate lesson in life. Though he was remiss in honoring his debt, Heidegger took much guidance from Kierkegaard on the nature and meaning of anxiety. According to the philosopher from the Black Forest, the experience of anxiety yanks us out of the crowd, and only by virtue of our being extricated from the herd (a feeling Heidegger describes as "homesickness") can we reenter into an authentic relation to our community.

For many of us, throughout our life we are forced to confront depression, a fire-breathing dragon. I enlisted Kierkegaard in our deliberation on the inexplicable sadness to retrieve a distinction between a psychological malady and

---

Anxiety is not simply a disrupting affect accompanied by sweaty palms and an increased pulse rate. It is a feeling with a message, one with an important cognitive component.

---

a spiritual illness, or, in the case at hand, between depression and despair. At one level, which Kierkegaard would
describe as "immediacy," we are swamped by moods and
feelings, but if we try, we can still manage to keep a part of
ourselves outside those feelings. No matter how hopeless
you might feel, Kierkegaard teaches, you still have a responsibility to reach through the pain and to care for and about
others even if you find it hard to care about yourself. Failing
to make that effort runs up the white flag on your moral
responsibilities, the point when we slip from depression, a
psychological malady, into the spiritual malady of despair.
In the chapter on depression and despair, we also pondered
how walking under what Julia Kristeva christened "the
black sun" can illuminate our absolute vulnerability in life
and expand our capacity for empathy.

From the chapter about death, we learned that Kierkegaard and Tolstoy underscored the fact that an abstract understanding of your mortality is a distant cry from a personal
grasp of what it means that there will come a time when there
will be no more time, when "all is over." Here the Kierkegaardian theme of the "self as a relation that relates itself to
itself" again looms. Philosophers—and people in general—
are of different minds when it comes to responding to the
question of how we should relate ourselves to our impending
doom. Many shrug—you have one life to live; don't waste it
morosely mulling over the end of that life. Kierkegaard, the

poet-philosopher who essentially gave us the category of "the individual," maintained that thinking of yourself as dead is good medicine. Earnest reflection on the meaning of our inevitable death, Kierkegaard promises, will allow every moment to become more valuable and endow finite issues with new and more powerful significance. Deeply appropriated, the idea of our death will help us avoid being sloppy in our relationships. If you have a spat, the existentialists implore, clear it up and make amends. Knowing that it is dust to dust will reprioritize our lives. Tolstoy concurs with Kierkegaard that a skull on the desk can reshuffle our deck of values, but as the head of a large family and an infinitely more social creature than his Danish counterpart, Tolstoy also intimated that the ubiquitous denial of death was partially responsible for the inauthentic personal relations of modern society.

In the chapter on depression and despair, we also pondered how walking under what Julia Kristeva christened "the black sun" can illuminate our absolute vulnerability in life and expand our capacity for empathy.

Existentialists are seldom included in ethics courses. Nevertheless, it is not just our relation to ourselves that we concentrated on throughout the text but also our relations with others. This is the very topic of morals. Sartre maintained that there is no objective way of distinguishing right from wrong, asserting that sacred texts and ethical theories could be used for or against almost any course of action. Sartre claims that your so-called gut feelings don't have any value until you act on them. Without us having a foundation with which to make decisions, our moral lives become fraught with anxiety. Targeting the Freudian notion of the unconscious, Sartre reminds us of the temptation to "bad faith," to deny our freedom and to treat ourselves as though we were both subjects and objects.

Earnest reflection on the meaning of our inevitable death, Kierkegaard promises, will allow every moment to become more valuable and endow finite issues with new and more powerful significance.

Like Kant, Kierkegaard assumes that anyone aiming to lead a moral life would have to walk through the fire of times when doing the right thing will incinerate their prospects for happiness. If Kierkegaard were to devise one of those "ethics workshops" so trendy today, or perhaps be appointed editor of the *New York Times Magazine*'s long-running Ethicist section, he would probably counsel that we don't require more knowledge or new skills of analysis to help us resist lying to get out of a tight spot. Instead, Kierkegaard recommends that we need to be able to cleave to the ethical-religious knowledge that we already possess, and by doing so we can ward off the temptation to talk ourselves into believing that the easy way is the right way. Make no mistake about it, Kierkegaard averred that the tendency to hoodwink ourselves into a willed ignorance is the major barrier to leading a moral life.

If Kierkegaard were to devise one of those "ethics workshops" so trendy today, or perhaps be appointed editor of the *New York Times Magazine*'s long-running Ethicist section, he would probably counsel that we don't require more knowledge or new skills of analysis to help us resist lying to get out of a tight spot.

Like Marx and Freud, Nietzsche regularly deconstructed so-called sacred conscience. So far as Nietzsche was concerned, morals and conscience did not come from on high. Nor did they spring out of reason. Ethicists today, such as philosopher Philip Kitcher, believe that ethics, just like everything else, is best understood in evolutionary terms. Given historical and current events, it might seem ironic, but according to Kitcher and his ilk, ethics are evolving toward increased and expanding circles of cooperation. Nietzsche concurred that our moral ideals were rolling stones gathering the moss of different and often antithetical meanings, but stones rolled along by the play of forces like the will to power. Nietzsche's method of investigation was philological: he tracked changes in values by detailing shifts in the meaning of moral terms. Today "good" has pacific overtones; however, in ancient times it was laden with martial connotations. Nietzsche raises the untimely question: What is the value of value? Like the utilitarians, whom he found utterly repugnant, Nietzsche believed that humans created morals, and our morals could enhance and/or poison culture. Nietzsche was wedded to the belief that over the course of history and through what he deemed the "slave revolt," the ascetic ideal had been erected as the moral touchstone. Given this criterion, for anything to be termed "good" it had to at least appear to involve an element of self-sacrifice. For example, I can't just charge forward and insist that I want to be the best; I have to adorn my ambitions in altruistic motives. I can decide to become a doctor or a lawyer, for instance, but I first have to at least present the pretense that I am primarily moved to help people—not because I crave challenges, wealth, and status in my community.

Nietzsche's rollicking writing gets under the skin and can make us attentive to the subterranean power interests possibly lurking behind our so-called better angels. Ironically enough, Nietzsche battled against the inward-gazing suspicious eye, and yet when you read him, you can't help but become a detective regarding your own motives. In addition to Nietzsche's nudging us to be strong enough to let things go beyond forgiveness to forgetting, these uplifting or at least cleansing doubts are moral lessons enough.

For anything to be termed "good" it had to at least appear to involve an element of self-sacrifice.

What, though, can the existentialists teach us about faith?

Kierkegaard agreed with Nietzsche—the self-proclaimed Anti-Christ—that God was dead, or at least faith in God was moribund. After a public fray with a popular newspaper, Kierkegaard, an inveterate walker, would be stalked by Copenhagen street urchins, teasingly yelling at him *"Enten/Eller"*—Either/Or. Either faith or unbelief. According to Kierkegaard, the choice between the sacred and the profane is not one that reason can make. Put another way, if you put all your faith in reason, you have made your choice. Conversely, where faith is concerned, it involves a terrible clash. This is the proverbial fallen tree on the path Kierkegaard repeatedly stresses. After all, is it any surprise that the groundswells of scientific knowledge have brought with it an ebb tide of faith? Matthew Arnold's plaintiff poem "Dover

Beach" speaks to the aftershocks of the collision between faith and reason. Here is the fourth stanza:

> *The Sea of Faith*
> *Was once, too, at the full, and round earth's shore* ·
> *Lay like the folds of a bright girdle furl'd.*
> *But now I only hear*
> *Its melancholy, long, withdrawing roar,*
> *Retreating, to the breath*
> *Of the night-wind, down the vast edges drear*
> *And naked shingles of the world.*

For those who still long to be awash in the sea of faith, Kierkegaard's most profound theological insight is his tethering of the possibility of faith and offense. In Kierkegaard's time and much more so in our own, there is a tendency to reduce religion to either a gauzy form of spirituality or to something akin to philosophy for dummies—good, uplifting, and yet untenable stories that would be better served by science and argument. Recall that for Kierkegaard faith is a paradoxical movement of giving up the world and expecting it back. To the extent that he talks about the object of faith, the idea that the eternal came into time and died is paradoxical, hardly something rationality can easily get into its head.

According to Kierkegaard, we can react one of two ways to the conflict between faith and reason. We can take offense and dismiss the conclusions rejected by the intellect, or reason can smilingly step aside and grant that faith surpasses understanding. In a late journal entry, Kierkegaard comments:

> In every generation, most people . . . live and die in the delusion that things keep on going, and that if it were granted to them to live longer, things would keep going onward in a continuing, straight forward ascent with more and more comprehension. How many experience at all the maturity of discovering that there comes a critical point where things turn around, when what matters from then on is an increasing comprehension that more and more comprehends that there is something that cannot be comprehended?[1]

Comprehending the importance of the incomprehensible would be reason's happy relation to the paradox of Christian faith.

Another chunk of wisdom to be extracted from the cavernous mines of Kierkegaard's writing is the notion that faith is not so much a matter of belief as it is a matter of how you relate to your unbelief. In one of Kierkegaard's shorter tracts, *Johnnas Cimacus, or De Omnibus Dubitandum Est*, our author noted that faith and doubt are not opposites because both are expressions of passionate concern. The decisive issue is this—when you find yourself

shaking your head incredulously at the mention of an all-
loving and all-knowing creator, do you pray to the God
you don't believe in for faith, or wave goodbye, convinced
that faith is a feeling that you either have or you don't? It is
common to hear a person say "I lost my faith," but from a
Kierkegaardian frame of reference, faith is not something
you lose. It is a possibility that you push away and then, after a time, feel as though it was something you passively lost
when in fact it was an essential something that you rejected.

Faith is not so much a matter of belief as it is a matter of
how you relate to your unbelief.

The how-to in this book is one of how to lead an authentic life in an inauthentic world. It would be dishonest
to pretend we succeeded in defining authenticity in the
way that we might be able to define a healthy heart. In his
Sincerity and Authenticity, Lionel Trilling undertakes the
Nietzschean labor of providing a genealogy of the terms
that comprise the title of his minor classic. According to
Trilling, authenticity was a child of the concept of sincerity,
which, in addition to honesty, was long understood to be
a full-fledged commitment to work, duty, and our station
in life. "It was the principle of civilization itself," Trilling
writes, "the principle which guaranteed the trait on which

the English most prided themselves, their sincerity, by which they meant their single-minded relations to things, to each other, and to themselves." Following Trilling, the concept of authenticity went through vicissitudes of meaning, in time being connected with something more organic and hostile to the ever-encroaching world of machines, technology, and the hegemony of the almighty dollar. Authenticity came to be seen as a matter of *being* as opposed to *having*.

It is natural to think that being masked was the polar opposite of authenticity. But Trilling reminds us that Nietzsche, the very individual who commanded "Become who you are," also maintained that "Every profound spirit needs a mask," for it appears "that all great things bestride the earth in monstrous and frightening masks in order to inscribe themselves in the hearts of humanity with eternal demands."

Other than Nietzsche, the existentialists associated authenticity with becoming your true self. The line of fracture that we walk in this book is one between thinking of your "true self" as a creation or as a discovery. Is there a deeper self that we were meant to discover and actualize, or is becoming yourself akin to an artistic creation, with the palette consisting of your culture, talents, feelings? Of course, the relation to ourselves that Kierkegaard deems authentic requires a hop, skip, and—in the end, as in all things—a giant leap of faith.

ACKNOWLEDGMENTS

Maybe thanklessness stems from the pride of wanting to be father to ourselves, from the desire to imagine that we have done everything on our own; either/or, my mentor, Philip Rieff, who pops up in the preceding pages and to whom I am eternally grateful, used to moan about what he termed "the iron law of ingratitude." And so it is with some trepidation, lest I forget to press someone's hand, that I acknowledge my debt to the people who have helped bring this book to fruition.

I am a cornerman in boxing. In terms of coaching, it is one of the most intense and intimate tasks in sports. So too in writing. I have been blessed to have a tight cadre of people working my corner. My agent, Jill Kneerim, provided both emotional support and literary guidance from the opening to the final bell. Dr. Beatrice Beebe knew better than I the inner roadblocks that I would face in trying to face myself in this endeavor. When I lost confidence, she was there and has always been there. My editor son, Philip Marino, performed as a gentle coach to the dad who coached him on the gridiron. I embrace him for his editorial comments and clarity of vision, but also for not tolerating his father's whining. I thank my son Paul, my brother, Thomas, and my brother of the spirit, Ned Rogers, for patiently listening to my bellyaching while gently pushing me forward. My wife, Susan, to whom this book is dedicated, has always been the first and last line of the editorial process in virtually everything I have written. My debt to her has no horizon.

Mark Tauber, publisher of HarperOne, was the prime mover behind this enterprise. His imagination and confidence in me set this project in motion; for that and more, I will always be grateful. I am much obliged to Miles Doyle, my highly astute and patient editor. Always flexible and gentle with his wise suggestions, Miles was able to discern connections that were out of my line of intellectual vision. I also want to express my appreciation to Eva Avery and Suzanne Quist for their deft work at shaping and burnishing the nuggets of wisdom that I was trying to articulate. I am beholden to Noah Greenberg for his discerning eye and generosity.

With my being a professor and director of the Hong Kierkegaard Library, there were umpteen times when my associate Eileen Shimota stepped in to deal with situations and help free me to find time to write. I am profoundly grateful for the interference she ran and for her enthusiastic encouragement.

NOTES

INTRODUCTION

1. David E. Cooper, *Existentialism* (Cambridge: Blackwell, 1993), 9.
2. See *Existentialism Basic Writings: Kierkegaard, Nietzsche, Heidegger, Sartre*, eds. Charles Guignon and Derk Pereboom (Indianapolis: Hackett Publishing Co., 1995).
3. Søren Kierkegaard, *The Sickness unto Death: A Christian Psychological Exposition for Upbuilding and Awakening*, ed. and trans. Howard V. Hong and Edna H. Hong (Princeton: Princeton Univ. Press, 1983), 13. Emphasizing the active and relational nature of the self, the quote continues: "the self is not the relation but is the relation's relating itself to itself."
4. Friedrich Nietzsche, *Ecce Homo*, trans. Duncan Large (Oxford: Oxford Univ. Press, 2007), 88.

5. Jean-Paul Sartre, *Nausea*, trans. Lloyd Alexander (New York: New Directions Publishing, 1964), 129.

6. Jean-Paul Sartre, *Being and Nothingness: A Phenomenological Essay on Ontology*, trans. Hazel E. Barnes (New York: Washington Square Press, 1984), 34.

7. Albert Camus, *The Myth of Sisyphus*, trans. J. O'Brien (New York: Vintage Books, 1955), 3.

8. See Søren Kierkegaard, *Two Ages: The Age of Revolution and the Present Age*, ed. and trans. Howard V. Hong and Edna H. Hong (Princeton: Princeton Univ. Press, 1978), 68–69.

9. Søren Kierkegaard, *Works of Love*, ed. and trans. Howard V. Hong and Edna H. Hong (Princeton: Princeton Univ. Press, 1995), 5.

CHAPTER 1: ANXIETY

1. E. M. Cioran, *The Trouble with Being Born*, trans. R. Howard (New York: Seaver Books, 1986), 84.

2. Søren Kierkegaard, *Kierkegaard's Journals and Papers*, ed. and trans. Howard V. Hong and Edna H. Hong (Bloomington: Indiana Univ. Press, 1978), 5:258 entry 5743 (V A 71, n.d., 1844).

3. Søren Kierkegaard, *Kierkegaard's Journals and Papers*, 6:72 entry 6274 (IX A 411, n.d., 1848).

4. Søren Kierkegaard, *Either/Or, Part I*, ed. and trans. Howard V. Hong and Edna H. Hong (Princeton: Princeton Univ. Press, 1987), 34.

5. Søren Kierkegaard, *Kierkegaard's Journals and Notebooks*, ed. Bruce H. Kirmmse (Princeton: Princeton Univ. Press, 2011), 4:230, Journal NB: 239.

6. Søren Kierkegaard, *The Concept of Anxiety: A Simple Psychologically Orienting Deliberation on the Dogmatic Issue of Hereditary Sin*, ed. & trans. R. Thomte (Princeton: Princeton Univ. Press, 1980), 160–61.

7. Kierkegaard, *The Concept of Anxiety*, 42.

8. Kierkegaard, *Kierkegaard's Journals and Papers*, 1:39 entry 94.

9. Kierkegaard, *The Concept of Anxiety*, 42.

10. Kierkegaard, *The Concept of Anxiety*, 161.

11. Kierkegaard, *The Concept of Anxiety*, 155.

12. Kierkegaard, *The Concept of Anxiety*, 155.

13. Kierkegaard, *The Concept of Anxiety*, 159.

14. Kierkegaard, *The Concept of Anxiety*, 159.

CHAPTER 2: DEPRESSION AND DESPAIR

1. Julia Kristeva, *Black Sun: Depression and Melancholia*, trans. Leon S. Roudiez (New York: Columbia Univ. Press, 1989).

2. Kierkegaard, *Either/Or, Part I*, 19.

3. Kierkegaard, *Kierkegaard's Journals and Papers*, 5:69 entry 5141 (1 A 161, n.d., 1836).

4. Kierkegaard, *Kierkegaard's Journals and Papers*, 6:306 entry 6603 (X^2 A 619, n.d., 1850).

5. Søren Kierkegaard, *Either/Or, Part II*, ed. and trans. Howard V. Hong and Edna H. Hong (Princeton: Princeton Univ. Press, 1990), 189.

6. Kierkegaard, *The Sickness unto Death*, 25.

7. Vincent A. McCarthy, *The Phenomenology of Moods in Kierkegaard* (Boston: Martinus Nijhoff, 1978), 86–87.

8. Kierkegaard, *The Sickness unto Death*, 13.

9. Kierkegaard, *The Sickness unto Death*, 19.

10. Kierkegaard, *Kierkegaard's Journals and Papers*, 5:334 entry 5913 (VII^1 A 126, n.d., 1846).

11. Søren Kierkegaard, "At a Graveside," in *Three Discourses on Imagined Occasions*, ed. and trans. Howard V. Hong and Edna H. Hong (Princeton: Princeton Univ. Press, 1993), 84.

12. Kierkegaard, "At a Graveside," 87.

13. Tim Farrington, *A Hell of Mercy: A Meditation on Depression and the Dark Night of the Soul* (San Francisco: HarperOne, 2009), 99.

14. Farrington, *A Hell of Mercy*, 99.

15. Linden Smith, "People Need to Grieve When Grieving Is in Order," *Star Tribune*, September 24, 2017.

CHAPTER 3: DEATH

1. Arthur Schopenhauer, *Parerga and Paralipomena: A Collection of Philosophical Essays*, trans. T. Bailey Saunders (New York: Cosimo Classics), 105.
2. Søren Kierkegaard, *Concluding Unscientific Postscript to Philosophical Fragments*, ed. and trans. Howard V. Hong and Edna H. Hong (Princeton: Princeton Univ. Press, 1992), 165.
3. Kierkegaard, "At a Graveside," 81.
4. William Barrett, *The Illusion of Technique* (Garden City, NY: Anchor Books, 1979), 258.

CHAPTER 4: AUTHENTICITY

1. Gail Sheehy, *Passages: Predictable Crises of Adult Life* (New York: Bantam Books, 1976), 364, 513 as quoted by Charles Taylor, *The Ethics of Authenticity* (Cambridge: Harvard Univ. Press, 1991), 44.
2. B. G. Yacobi, "The Limits of Authenticity," *Philosophy Now* 92 (September–October 2012).
3. Søren Kierkegaard, *Works of Love*, ed. and trans. Howard V. Hong and Edna H. Hong (Princeton: Princeton Univ. Press, 1995), 209.

4. Friedrich Nietzsche, *The Gay Science*, trans. Walter Kaufmann (New York: Vintage Books, 1974), 218.
5. Mike W. Martin, *Self-Deception and Morality* (Lawrence, Kansas: Univ. Press of Kansas, 1986), 75.
6. Taylor, *The Ethics of Authenticity*, 91.

CHAPTER 5: FAITH

1. Camus, *The Myth of Sisyphus*, 121, 123.
2. Arthur Schopenhauer, *Parerga and Paralipomena*, trans. E. F. J. Payne (Oxford: Clarendon Press, 1974), 2:298–99.
3. Søren Kierkegaard, *Fear and Trembling/Repetition*, ed. and trans. Howard V. Hong and Edna H. Hong (Princeton: Princeton Univ. Press, 1983), 15.
4. Kierkegaard, *The Sickness unto Death*, 53.
5. Kierkegaard, *The Concept of Anxiety*, 78–79.
6. Kierkegaard, *The Sickness unto Death*, 117–18.
7. Kierkegaard, *Concluding Unscientific Postscript*, 201.
8. Kierkegaard, *The Concept of Anxiety*, 139–40.
9. Kierkegaard, *The Concept of Anxiety*, 71.

CHAPTER 6: MORALITY

1. Jean-Paul Sartre, *Existentialism Is a Humanism*, ed. John Kulka, trans. Carol Macomber (New Haven: Yale Univ. Press, 2007).

2. Sartre, *Being and Nothingness*, 89.

3. Jean-Paul Sartre, "Existentialism," in *Existentialism and Human Emotions*, trans. Bernard Frechtman (New York: Citadel Press, 1985), 34.

4. Friedrich Nietzsche, *On the Genealogy of Morals*, trans. Walter Kaufmann and R. J. Hollingdale, ed. Walter Kaufmann (New York: Vintage Books, 1989), 31.

5. Nietzsche, *On the Genealogy of Morals*, 49.

6. Friedrich Nietzsche, *Writings of Nietzsche, Volume II*, ed. Anthony Uyl (Ontario: Devoted Publishing, 2016), 101.

7. J. S. Mill, "On Civilization," in *Dissertations and Discussion: Political, Philosophical and Historical* (London: John W. Parker and Son, 1859), vol. I, 180–81.

8. Nietzsche, *On the Genealogy of Morals*, 25.

9. Nietzsche, *On the Genealogy of Morals*, 66.

10. Nietzsche, *On the Genealogy of Morals*, 39.

11. Kierkegaard, *Kierkegaard's Journals and Papers*, 1:285, Addition to 85:8.

12. Kierkegaard, *The Sickness unto Death*, 91.

13. Kierkegaard, *The Sickness unto Death*, 94.

14. Kierkegaard, *The Sickness unto Death*, 94.

15. Gordon Marino, "What's the Use of Regret," *New York Times*, November 12, 2016, SR8.

CHAPTER 7: LOVE

1. Albert Camus, *The Fall*, trans. Justin O'Brien (New York: Vintage Books, 1984), 28.
2. Kierkegaard, *Works of Love*, 89.
3. Fyodor Dostoevsky, *Notes from Underground*, ed. and trans. Michael R. Katz (New York: W. W. Norton, 1989), 59–60.
4. Dostoevsky, *Notes from Underground*, 66–67.
5. Dostoevsky, *Notes from Underground*, 82–83.
6. Dostoevsky, *Notes from Underground*, 84–85.

EPILOGUE

1. Kierkegaard, *Kierkegaard's Journals and Notebooks*, 6:134, 225, Journal NB: 12.

BIBLIOGRAPHY

Bakewell, Sarah. *At the Existentialist Café: Freedom, Being, and Apricot Cocktails*. New York: Other Press, 2016.

Barrett, William. *The Illusion of Technique*. Garden City, NY: Anchor Books, 1979.

Becker, Ernest. *The Denial of Death*. New York: Free Press, 1973.

Camus, Albert. *The Fall*. Translated by Justin O'Brien. New York: Vintage Books, 1984.

———. *The Myth of Sisyphus*. Translated by Justin O'Brien. New York: Vintage Books, 1955.

———. *The Stranger*. Translated by Matthew Ward. New York: Vintage Books, 1989.

Cioran, E. M. *The Trouble with Being Born*. Translated by Richard Howard. New York: Seaver Books, 1986.

Cooper, David E. *Existentialism*. Cambridge: Blackwell, 1993.

DeLillo, Don. *White Noise.* New York: Penguin Books, 1986.

Dostoevsky, Fyodor. *Notes from Underground.* Edited and translated by Michael R. Katz. New York: W. W. Norton, 1989.

Farrington, Tim. *A Hell of Mercy: A Meditation on Depression and the Dark Night of the Soul.* San Francisco: HarperOne, 2009.

Guignon, Charles, and Derk Pereboom, eds. *Existentialism: Basic Writings: Kierkegaard, Nietzsche, Heidegger, Sartre.* Indianapolis: Hackett Publishing, 1995.

Heidegger, Martin. *Being and Time.* Translated by John MacQuarrie and Edward Robinson. New York: Harper Perennial Modern Thought, 1962.

Horwitz, Allan V., and Jerome C. Wakefield. *The Loss of Sadness: How Psychiatry Transformed Normal Sorrow into Depressive Disorder.* Oxford: Oxford University Press, 2007.

Kierkegaard, Søren. *Concluding Unscientific Postscript to "Philosophical Fragments."* Edited and translated by Howard V. Hong and Edna H. Hong. Princeton: Princeton University Press, 1992.

———. *Either/Or, Part I.* Edited and translated by Howard V. Hong and Edna H. Hong. Princeton: Princeton University Press, 1987.

———. *Either/Or, Part II.* Edited and translated by Howard V. Hong and Edna H. Hong. Princeton: Princeton University Press, 1990.

——. *Fear and Trembling/Repetition*. Edited and translated by Howard V. Hong and Edna H. Hong. Princeton: Princeton University Press, 1983.

——. *Kierkegaard's Journals and Notebooks*. Edited by Bruce H. Kirmmse. Vols. 1–6. Princeton: Princeton University Press, 2007–12.

——. *Søren Kierkegaard's Journals and Papers*. Edited and translated by Howard V. Hong and Edna H. Hong. Vols. 1–7. Bloomington: Indiana University Press, 1967–78.

——. *The Concept of Anxiety: A Simple Psychologically Orienting Deliberation on the Dogmatic Issue of Hereditary Sin*. Edited and translated by Reidar Thomte in collaboration with Albert B. Anderson. Princeton: Princeton University Press, 1980.

——. *The Sickness unto Death: A Christian Psychological Exposition for Upbuilding and Awakening*. Edited and translated by Howard V. Hong and Edna H. Hong. Princeton: Princeton University Press, 1983.

——. "At a Graveside." In *Three Discourses on Imagined Occasions*, edited and translated by Howard V. Hong and Edna H. Hong. Princeton: Princeton University Press, 1993.

——. *Works of Love*. Edited and translated by Howard V. Hong and Edna H. Hong. Princeton: Princeton University Press, 1995.

Kristeva, Julia. *Black Sun*. Translated by Leon S. Roudiez. New York: Columbia University Press, 1989.

Marino, Gordon, ed. *Basic Writings of Existentialism.* New York: Modern Library, 2004.

——. *Kierkegaard in the Present Age.* Marquette: Marquette University Press, 2001.

Martin, Mike W. *Self-Deception and Morality.* Lawrence, Kansas: University Press of Kansas, 1986.

May, Rollo. *The Meaning of Anxiety.* New York: W. W. Norton, 2015.

McCarthy, Vincent A. *The Phenomenology of Moods in Kierkegaard.* Boston: Martinus Nijhoff, 1978.

Nietzsche, Friedrich. *Ecce Homo.* Translated by Duncan Large. Oxford: Oxford University Press, 2007.

——. *On the Genealogy of Morals.* Edited by Walter Kaufmann. Translated by Walter Kaufmann and R. J. Hollingdale. New York: Vintage Books, 1989.

——. *The Gay Science.* Translated by Walter Kaufmann. New York: Vintage Books, 1974.

Norris, Kathleen. *Acedia and Me: A Marriage, Monks, and a Writer's Life.* New York: Riverhead Books, 2010.

Rieff, Philip. *Freud: The Mind of the Moralist.* Chicago: University of Chicago Press, 1959.

——. *The Triumph of the Therapeutic: Uses of Faith After Freud.* New York: Harper & Row, 1966.

Sartre, Jean-Paul. *Being and Nothingness: A Phenomenological Essay on Ontology.* Translated by Hazel E. Barnes. New York: Washington Square Press, 1984.

——. *Existentialism Is a Humanism.* Edited by John Kulka.

Translated by Carol Macomber. New Haven: Yale University Press, 2007.

——. *Nausea*. Translated by Lloyd Alexander. New York: New Directions Publishing, 1964.

Schopenhauer, Arthur. *Parerga and Paralipomena*. Translated by E. F. J. Payne. Oxford: Clarendon Press, 1974.

Sheehy, Gail. *Passages: Predictable Crises of Adult Life*. New York: Bantam Books, 1976.

Smith, Emily Esfahani. *The Power of Meaning: Crafting a Life That Matters*. New York: Crown, 2017.

Taylor, Charles. *The Ethics of Authenticity*. Cambridge: Harvard University Press, 1991.

Tillich, Paul. *The Courage to Be*. New Haven: Yale University Press, 1952.

Tolstoy, Leo. *The Death of Ivan Ilych and Other Stories*. Translated by Rosemary Edmonds. New York: Penguin Classics, 1989.

Watts, Alan W. *The Wisdom of Insecurity: A Message for an Age of Anxiety*. New York: Vintage Books, 2011.

Yalom, Irvin D. *Love's Executioner and Other Tales of Psychotherapy*. New York: Basic Books, 2012.

ABOUT THE AUTHOR

Gordon Marino is a professor of philosophy and the director of the Hong Kierkegaard Library at St. Olaf College in Northfield, Minnesota. Professor Marino took his doctorate from the Committee on Social Thought at the University of Chicago. Before coming to St. Olaf in 1995, he taught at Harvard, Yale, and Virginia Military Institute.

A recipient of the Richard J. Davis Ethics Award for excellence in writing on ethics and the law, Marino is the author of *Kierkegaard in the Present Age*, coeditor of *The Cambridge Companion to Kierkegaard*, and editor of the Modern Library's *Basic Writings of Existentialism* and *Ethics: The Essential Writings*. In addition to scholarly publications, Marino's essays have appeared in the *New York Times*, *Newsweek*, *The Atlantic*, *The Wall Street Journal*, and many other national and international publications.

A former boxer, Dr. Marino has been a USA Boxing

coach since 1995. He was head coach of boxing at Virginia Military Institute and currently trains both amateurs and professionals in Minnesota. He is also an award-winning boxing writer for, among other venues, *The Wall Street Journal*.